FBI Family Story

The Ouellette Legacy

I0540719

Mark Ouellette

ANCHOR & INK
PUBLISHING

Melbourne, Florida

Cover design by Lisa D. Vest & Mark Ouellette
Edited by Lisa D. Vest
Interior layout by Heather Mize

Published by Anchor & Ink Publishing
P.O. Box 360014
Melbourne, FL 32936
www.anchorandinkpublishing.com

An FBI Family Story / Mark Ouellette. — 1st ed.

978-1-969007-04-0 (ebook)
978-1-969007-05-7 (paperback)
978-1-969007-06-4(hardcover)

Printed in the United States of America

Dedication

I would like to dedicate this book to my mother, Lois Morgan Ouellette, and father, John Norman Ouellette, who made it all possible.

"Always be respectful and courteous to anyone and everyone you meet! You never know what doors it may open!"

John Norman Ouellette

Table of Contents

FOREWORD

While I was playing quarterback for the Grafton High School varsity football team during the fall 1976 season, Special Agent John Ouellette, whose son, Mark, played fullback and is author of this book, *FBI Family Story*, volunteered to film our football games for the coaches and players to review on Monday afternoons following the games.

Mr. Ouellette excelled in football and basketball while attending North High School in Worcester, Massachusetts, prior to entering the Army Air Corps in 1945, attending Holy Cross College in 1947 and then joining the FBI in 1952.

While filming our football games during the 1976 season, we would not realize until the end of the season that he had documented the first Grafton High School undefeated varsity football season and the team's first trip to the Super Bowl.

FBI Family Story offers an opportunity to learn about the legacy created by Special Agent John Ouellette and his wife, FBI File Clerk Lois Morgan Ouellette, and their seven children.

Steve Spagnuolo
Defense Coordinator
Kansas City Chiefs

CHAPTER 1

John Norman Ouellette

L-R Irene, John Sr., Edna

John Ouellette was more than an FBI agent; he was an inspiration and role model. He and our mother, Lois Morgan Ouellette, created a life that focused on family values, morals, the Catholic Church, and family fun.

Born October 18, 1926, in Worcester, Massachusetts, to John and Florina (Moreau) Ouellette, John Norman Ouellette came into this world, where it would meet him with challenges, opportunities, and sometimes a sense of fate.

His father, a professional boxer, was known as "Kid Willetts." During the early years of his professional boxing career, Kid Willetts worked as a florist in Fall River, Massachusetts. He became the lightweight champion in 1909. After meeting, then marrying Florina Moreau, also from Fall River, he and his new wife moved to Worcester, Massachusetts, where he continued boxing and took a job as a skilled leather worker at Graton & Knight Leather Company. He became a member of the Local 46 United & Leather Union. Kid Willett made additional money boxing

Kid Willetts Official
Promotional Poster

bare knuckled for gambling purposes in open fields in the Fall River and Worcester County areas.

Kid Ouellette
1909 Lightweight Champion

At the Graton & Knight leather factory where he was employed, there was a small gym where he taught boxing classes. Later in life, he worked as a security officer at the same leather factory.

Florina Moreau Ouellette was a French Canadian dedicated to family and the Catholic Church. She was born in Fall River, Massachusetts, and as a young adult, went to work at a thread manufacturing factory in Fall River. This was where she met and married our grandfather, Kid Willett. At some point, they moved to Chrome Street and later to Wall Street in Worcester. I remember spending time with her as a young child while in Worcester and on Cape Cod in the early and mid-1960s.

John Ouellette Wearing
His Dad's Boxing Gloves

Our dad, John Norman Ouellette, grew up on Wall Street in Worcester, Massachusetts, along with his older sisters Edna and Irene. Dad was a member of St. Joseph's Catholic Church in Worcester, where he served as an altar boy. He often talked about how he and the other kids in the Wall Street area played touch football, marbles, kick the can, hide and seek, and catch with a baseball. I have no doubt this is why he organized and played these games with us when we were children.

I recently had the honor of meeting one of Dad's childhood friends while writing the first chapter of this book. Her name is Beatrice Mailett. She was six years old when Dad was eight. Beatrice, at the youthful age of ninety-four, remembers Dad and the Wall Street neighborhood well. Beatrice told me she always knew that our dad would go a long way in life.

Dad used to deliver newspapers when he was twelve. During the hurricane of 1938, he was stuck at a customer's house and had to wait for the storm to calm down. When the eye of the storm came over Worcester, it gave him enough time to get back on his bike and head home. It was also at age twelve that he was temporarily knocked out while sledding down a hill near his home during a snowstorm.

As a young boy, Dad often went to the Worcester YMCA to play basketball and work out. He also enjoyed going there on Saturdays to watch the *Flash Gordon* series, *The Three Stooges, Zorro, and Tarzan movies* presented on a 16-millimeter film projector. He also saw the Three Stooges perform live at the Plymouth Theater on Main Street in Worcester in 1935.

**John Sr. Ouellette
Age 8-9**

Dad and his older sisters, Irene and Edna, occasionally spent hot summer afternoons at Indian Lake in Worcester. He told me on more than one occasion about an incident that took place at the lake, where he had bumped his head on a rock and was underwater drowning. With vivid recollection, he remembered floating out and above his body while watching his sisters and a lifeguard pull him out of the water and perform resuscitation. He described this experience as being peaceful and comfortable while feeling physically complete, as though his body was only a "shell" containing his soul.

After a short time observing the resuscitation efforts below, he suddenly returned to his physical body "with a jolt" and started coughing up water. I have no doubt that this experience contributed to his commitment to the Catholic Church and the belief in life continuing after death.

At age ten, I had a similar experience at a hospital while on vacation in Florida during the summer of 1968. I will share my experience and the medical report later in this book. Ironically, Dad ended up working part time as a lifeguard at Indian Lake while attending Holy Cross College in Worcester.

There was a small shop on Grafton Street in Worcester, from the 1940s through the 1980s, run by a man named Charlie. This was a place where Dad and other kids in the neighborhood went for sodas, ice cream, and to socialize.

John Sr. Ouellette Age 15

I had the opportunity to meet Charlie in 1967 when we went back to Worcester to attend Dad's mother's funeral. Also attending the funeral and wake were my older brothers, John Jr. and James. Mom stayed home in Avon Lake with Paul, Marie, and Neal. Richard had not been born yet. It was my first experience attending a wake and a funeral. We stayed at our grandmother's house during the 1967 funeral trip. This was the only time I ever saw the inside of the home where Dad had grown up as a child and young adult.

Dad attended North High School in Worcester, Massachusetts, where he excelled in football and basketball. I remember him telling me that wide receivers never caught many footballs but did a lot of blocking. Dad taught me how to shoot a basketball using one hand to balance the ball and the other hand to push the ball. The Worcester Public Schools inducted him into the Athletic Hall of Fame a few years before he passed away in 2015.

John Sr. Ouellette

On Saturday, November 28, 1942, Dad, fourteen, along with his sisters Edna and Irene, attended the Holy Cross and Boston College football game at Fenway Park in Boston. In one of the greatest college football upsets of its time, Holy Cross beat Boston College by the score of 55-12. Because of the route, a Boston College bowl game party scheduled at the Coconut Grove Restaurant and Night Club that evening was canceled.

Many of the Holy Cross football fans who attended the game went to Coconut Grove to celebrate the historic upset and win. Many of these fans and others at Coconut Grove died that evening in a tragic fire. The Coconut Grove fire resulted in the deaths of 492 people. Many consider it the deadliest nightclub fire in US history and the second deadliest building fire in US history.

John Sr. # 23 North HS Football Championship

John Ouellette Sr. North HS Basketball Championship Team

Occasionally, Dad talked about how his sisters, Edna and Irene had left the Coconut Grove early that evening before the tragic fire because he was too young to stay out late and needed to be home early as he had church and family obligations the next morning. When telling this story, Dad often concluded by stating, "We all may not be here today had they stayed at the Coconut Grove later into that evening."

Dad graduated from North High School in early February 1945 and entered active duty in the US Army Air Corps on February 24, 1945. Like many young men of the day, he took accelerated courses that enabled him to graduate early so he could join the military and fight for our country during WWII. During his enlistment, the US Army transitioned him from the Army Air Corps to the Regular Army. Dad received training to become a belly turret machine gunner on B17 Bombers and a machine gun controller using electronic sights and joysticks on B29 Bombers. In addition, he trained and became a Crash Firefighter 383 and a Military Firefighter.

John Sr. Army AirCorps
Photo 1945

Occasionally, I asked Dad if he had ever shot down any Japanese planes. He would respond with, "Had we not dropped the atomic bombs on Japan, we all may not be here today!"

Dad told me about how they were trained to drop a special bomb. He pointed out that there were sixty-five bomber crews trained to drop these special weapons, and that it was not a complicated process. He explained, "Once the plane arrived at the drop location, the crew would release the bomb and quickly fly upward and away as fast as possible."

They were told to wear special eye-protective glasses and not to look down. The pilot of the Boeing B-27 Superfortress bomber used in this mission was Colonel Paul Tibbets. He nicknamed the bomber Enola Gay after his mother, Enola Gay Tibbets. Because of the intensity of kamikaze missions being conducted by Japanese pilots, the United States needed to train backup crews to be sure there were bombers and trained crews available to conduct the mission on the

John Sr. Ouellette
Toyko, Japan
March 1946

7

planned dates. Ultimately, it was the Enola Gay that dropped the first bomb on Hiroshima on August 6 and the second on Nagasaki on August 9, 1945, ultimately forcing the Japanese to surrender.

**John Sr. Watching General MacArthur Entering
Meiji Building Toyko, Japan 1946**

Following the Japanese surrender, Dad spent the rest of his military service with the US Occupational Forces in Japan. It is interesting to point out that he served in both the US Army Air Corps and Regular Army, allowing him the opportunity to receive two honorable discharges from the military.

While in Tokyo, Japan, on April 5, 1946, Dad was driving down the street and noticed soldiers and photographers gathering outside of the Meiji Building, headquarters of the Pacific Air Command and the Fifth Air Force. He parked his car and stood outside with other onlookers, and soon after, General Douglas MacAurthur arrived by automobile. MacAurthur was attending the opening meeting of the Four-Power Control Council. The press took a picture of MacArthur as he entered the building and the photo was published in a Japanese newspaper. In the photo, Dad is standing and watching MacArthur as he heads towards the steps of the building.

Dad occasionally mentioned that he had begun smoking cigarettes while stationed in Japan. The government delivered cases of cigarettes to the occupying American troops. There was not much to do in occupied Japan as the Japanese honored the surrender to America and caused little or no trouble. Playing cards and smoking cigarettes became popular with many of the American troops. Dad sometimes joked about the fact that he should sue the government for causing his addiction to cigarette smoking.

After reviewing Dad's Enlisted Record and Report of Separation Honorable Discharge documents, I learned he received the Good Conduct Medal, World War II Victory Medal, Asiatic Pacific Campaign Medal and Army of Occupation Medal. He, like so many other soldiers who served during WWII, received a personal thank-you letter from President Harry Truman.

Following military service, Dad attended Holy Cross College in Worcester, Massachusetts. Tuition was covered through his use of the GI Bill. He attended Holy Cross College from 1947 to 1951 and earned a Bachelor of Science degree, *magna cum laude*.

While attending Holy Cross College, he got to know Bob Cousy and occasionally play in some casual "pick-up" basketball games at the Holy Cross gym during the basketball off season.

John Sr. Lifeguard

At Holy Cross College, Dad also worked as a lifeguard at Indian Lake. He and his friends occasionally went to Coney Island Hot Dogs, down the hill from the school's campus. He carved his initials into the wood at the booth he and his friends frequented. His initials are still visible today. This was a practice allowed at the time and well preserved by the owners.

**John Sr. & Aunt Caroline
Holy Cross Graduation 1951**

Following his graduation from Holy Cross College, Dad joined the Federal Bureau of Investigation. He went to Quantico, Virginia, where he completed his training in 1951. He worked for the FBI from July 1951 until his retirement in July 1977.

In 1957, Dad attended the US Army Language School in Monterey, California, where he learned to speak Romanian. Hoover wanted to have at least one active agent in the FBI who could speak an existing foreign language for potential interrogation purposes.

It is interesting to point out that FBI agents often received reassignment to different parts of the country to avoid becoming too familiar in any given location. It was a little easier to manage in large cities where agents could move to multiple locations in and around the city and "quietly" blend in. This was the case for our family when he was stationed in Cleveland, Ohio. Our family moved around the Cleveland area four times between 1958 and 1965.

**Dad FBI Training
Quantico, VA 1951**

After completing his training, Dad was assigned to offices in Detroit, Michigan, Knoxville, Tennessee, New York City, Monterey, California, Cleveland, Ohio, Washington, DC, and Boston, Massachusetts. While in Washington, DC, he served as a supervisor in the Domestic Intelligence Division and oversaw the acceptance or denying of any potential FBI investigations for the entire East Coast of the United States. During his time in Washington, J. Edgar Hoover considered Dad to be a member of his informal "Top Ten."

John Sr. with His Mother Following Completion of FBI Training, Quantico, VA

Mr. Hoover's office was on the top floor of the FBI Headquarters in Washington, a strategic location where he could see his agents enter or depart the building. Dad's office was below on the next floor along with the other "Top Ten," also strategically located where they could see anyone who entered or left the building.

Dad shared with me a story about a young new agent arriving at the Washington FBI Headquarters wearing a purple tie. Hoover called Dad immediately and asked, "John, look out the window. Is he one of our agents?"

Dad replied, "Yes, Mr. Hoover."

Hoover responded, "John, take care of it."

Dad quickly made his way down to the lobby and brought the agent to his office, where he kept extra shirts, suits, and ties. Dad knew well what Hoover expected his agents to wear while on the job.

Hoover wanted agents to blend in and avoid the spotlight. He expected agents to wear conservative suits and drive ordinary cars. Agents should not "stand out" in the community. Dad gave the agent one of his suits and a tie that he kept in his office for these kinds of situations. Unfortunately, the next day, the agent received a transfer to the FBI Headquarters in Butte, Montana. This meant that the agent, along with his wife and children, would also live in Butte, Montana. Hoover was known for sending agents he deemed to be troublesome to isolated and less attractive areas around the country. Butte, Montana, was one of those locations.

Dad, and the other agents and staff at the FBI Headquarters in Washington, were exceptionally polite and respectful to Hoover's top executive secretary, Helen Gandy. According to Dad, Helen Gandy was the most powerful and influential person in the FBI after J. Edgar Hoover. Whenever Dad had a meeting with Hoover, he would bring a box of candy to give to Helen. Often, when a particular agent had a meeting with Hoover, they would remind each other, "Don't forget the Gandy candy."

Anytime Dad met with Hoover, he noticed the shoes of someone hiding behind the curtains. He knew it was Hoover's assistant Director Clyde Tolson, who thought he was secretly listening in on the meeting. Agents often joked behind Tolson's back about his supposedly poor surveillance skills, especially considering he was the FBI's second-in-command.

While working at the Washington, DC headquarters, certain agents were asked to come into the office on weekends and take the place of Mr. Hoover so he could enjoy time off. There was a TV in the break room so agents could watch the news along with a red telephone Hoover had installed, providing a direct line to any agents covering for him when he wanted to check in.

On Sundays and if "things were quiet," Dad would watch the Washington Redskins football game. It was already planned that if the red phone were to ring, agents would first turn the TV off before answering the phone. On more than one occasion, the phone rang, and Dad turned off the TV and answered the phone, "Hello Mr. Hoover."

Hoover would first ask, "John, are there any issues or concerns?" and then ask, "John, is the TV on? Are any of the agents watching the football game?"

Dad responded honestly. "No, Mr. Hoover, the TV is off!"

During the winter of 1972, Dad requested a transfer to the Boston, Massachusetts FBI Headquarters. He informed Hoover that he understood this was a step down from such a prominent position, but wanted to spend his last years working out of the Boston office and living near Worcester, where he had grown up. Hoover granted the transfer request and informed Dad he was saddened by his departure and wished him the best of luck. It was this transfer that brought our family to Grafton, Massachusetts. Moving to Grafton allowed for a close commute to the Boston office and a nice small town to continue raising seven children.

It is no secret that J. Edgar Hoover and President Richard Nixon did not get along well. While in Washington, Dad was one of the go-between agents who brought messages back and forth between Hoover and Nixon. Many of these messages were verbal and not written on paper. Hoover and Nixon did everything possible to avoid face-to-face communication. Dad thought it was rather "humorous" and somewhat "intriguing" that the two most powerful men in the country could not sit down and have a direct conversation.

After retiring from the FBI, Dad became a security manager at Raytheon Company where he supervised the security for the facilities producing the Hawk and Patriot missiles. His office was in Lexington, Massachusetts. While at Raytheon, he served two years in Saudi Arabia, overseeing the security for American citizens employed by Raytheon and the transport of Patriot and Hawk missiles to their top-secret set-up locations. After returning from Saudi Arabia, he oversaw security for the Raytheon facilities in Lexington, Bedford, and Marlborough, Massachusetts.

Dad was a member of the Society of Former Special Agents of the FBI, the American Legion Post 0462 in Boston, Massachusetts, and the Holy Cross College Alumni Association.

Dad was a quiet and modest person by nature and was willing to help anyone at any time. He dedicated his life to family and career. Our parents shared their morals and values through daily life, example, and natural role modeling. When Dad met Mom, who worked for the FBI as a high-level security file clerk at the Knoxville, Tennessee office, it was the beginning of an amazing adventure that I am proud to write about in this book.

CHAPTER 2

Lois Morgan Ouellette

On November 11, 1930, the Morgan family welcomed their third child, Lois Lillian Morgan. Her parents, Andrew J. and Althea (Houser) Morgan, lived in Pikeville, Tennessee, then later moved to nearby Dayton, Tennessee. Mom had two brothers, Wendell and Glenn, along with an older sister, Clarice.

Our mother's grandmother, Nora, was a full-blooded Cherokee Indian. I remember meeting her on a few occasions while visiting our relatives in Tennessee during the 1960s. Nora must have been in her upper 80s. She lived in a one-room log cabin with no electricity and used an outdoor water well that required hand cranking to retrieve water.

My grandmother, Althea, told me a story passed down to her about how the Morgans of Morgan Springs, a small village between Pikeville and Dayton, joined the Union Army to fight against slavery during the Civil War. She told me that the Morgan boys who enlisted in the Union Army had to be careful when returning home while on leave. It was the duty of Confederate soldiers to search for Southerners who had joined the Union Army and were attempting to visit family and friends during leave.

There were two Morgan boys who were back home visiting their families when a group of Rebels arrived in Morgan Springs. The young men quickly hid in a bean field, covering themselves with vines and leaves to avoid capture. Many of these Rebel squads shot these "traitors" on the spot.

During the 1830s and 1840s, the people living in Morgan Springs and Dayton, Tennessee, experienced firsthand the death and devastation caused by the Indian Removal Act. Many Cherokee Indians were found lying on the ground, weak and left to die along the section of the Trail that passed right through Morgan Springs and Dayton.

Thousands of Native Americans died during this period of history. President Andrew Jackson signed the Indian Removal Act into law on May 18, 1830. The act demanded that all Indians must relocate onto lands west of the Mississippi River in exchange for new Indian land.

Our mother enjoyed sharing stories about her childhood. She once told me about how she and other children in the Morgan Springs area attended taffy pulls. Taffy pulls were an opportunity for local families to gather and socialize on Saturday nights and occasionally Sunday afternoons following church. My mother and her family were Baptists.

As described by my mother, to make this delicious homemade taffy, the parents would mix the ingredients together and allow the children to pull and stretch the taffy before placing it on wax paper to settle and dry. The ingredients included white sugar, corn syrup, butter, cornstarch, and water along with a dash of salt, vanilla extract, and almond extract. Once the taffy was ready, the children then took a piece, placed it on a small piece of wax paper and smashed it or broke it into small bite-size pieces. You had to be careful where you left any uneaten taffy, as it was rather attractive to ants.

Mom attended a one-room schoolhouse in Morgan Springs. There was only one teacher responsible for teaching all the students, grades one through eight. Mom carried her lunch to school in an empty lard can. In the winter, her mother would give her two hot baked potatoes to carry in her pockets to keep her hands warm while walking to school. School lunches usually comprised a piece of freshly baked bread and a chunk of cheese. Depending on the time of year, she brought some locally grown fruit. This might include blueberries, strawberries, blackberries, apples, peaches, or plums, depending on what was in season.

Lois Morgan Ouellette 4th from R
One Room School House Grades 1-8 Pikeville, TN

People living in the area had access to fresh spring water drawn from Morgan Springs. Morgan Springs water was popular with the locals and visitors, especially those staying at the Morgan Springs Hotel. I remember my mom telling me that one hot summer day when she was a young teenager, she and a few of her friends "got drunk" by consuming too much spring water. Mom said that they were actually "imitating drunk adults" they would see at local gatherings and square dances.

Prior to the Indian Removal Act, Native Americans in the area often talked about the "magical powers" of the water drawn from the natural spring that became known as Morgan Springs.

By the late 1800s and early 1900s, resort-style hotels were being built in and around Tennessee, advertising the fresh air and healthy spring water. The first hotel built at Morgan Springs was completed in the late 1800s and called the Morgan Springs Hotel. The hotel provided summer visitors with an escape from the heat and pollution found in the cities. Many businessmen from Chattanooga and Dayton brought their families to the Morgan Springs Hotel on weekends or for weeks at a time during the summer.

Mom remembered attending special events held at the Morgan Springs Hotel when she was a child. There was usually a musical band consisting of an acoustic guitar player, a fiddle player, and other members who played the washboard, cowbells, and spoons. These events usually included a goat or pig roast served with corn on the cob, green "pinch" beans, and watermelon.

One of my mother's great uncles owned over 400 goats. These goats kept the entire Morgan Springs Mountain free of weeds and brush. He also donated or sold his goats for some of the local celebrations. On more than one occasion, Mom brought up the fact that the Fourth of July was the most celebrated time of the year. People lit firecrackers and shot guns into the air.

The Morgan Springs Hotel sat at the top of a hill, and there was a crank cable device that a person could use to transport buckets of water from the spring to the hotel. This "technology" impressed the children, who had fun fetching water for the hotel staff. Mom told me that the hotel staff had no issues with the children doing their labor.

My mother and grandmother often talked about the many events that took place at a building on the Morgan Springs Hotel property called Katydid. The Katydid was a special building with large openings allowing for fresh air and cool mountain breezes. It was a place where guests and locals could be comfortable playing cards, knitting, listening to music, reading books and enjoying hotel-sponsored activities. Women enjoyed gathering at the Katydid to play cards and make quilts while the children played. I remember visiting my grandmother in the mid-1980s and asking her what her favorite memory was while growing up in the Morgan Springs area. She quickly responded with a tear in her eye, "Going to the Katydid!"

The Morgan Springs Hotel was where many of the participants involved with the Scopes Monkey Trial stayed in July 1925. This historic event began on July 10, 1925, in Dayton, Tennessee, when John Thomas Scopes, a young high school science teacher, was accused of teaching evolution in violation of Tennessee state law. The law stated that to teach any theory that denies the story of Divine Creation as taught by the Bible and to teach that man had descended from a lower order of animals was committing a misdemeanor.

Following the arrest of Scopes, the American Civil Liberties Union came to defend John Thomas Scopes. Also defending Scopes was Clarence Darrow, a famous lawyer of the day. After learning about the case and the attack on Christian fundamentalism, William Jennings Bryan, a three-time Democratic presidential candidate and fundamentalist hero, volunteered to assist in the prosecution, setting the stage for one of the most famous trials in American history.

My grandmother remembered experiencing all the excitement and witnessing the well-trained monkey dressed in a suit being paraded and exhibited outside the Dayton courthouse during the proceedings. On one occasion, my grandmother was able to sit in and observe the proceedings. She told me it was hot and uncomfortable in the courthouse.

Another memorable event was when the circus came to town. It was exciting to see the elephants cross over the mountain along with the other animals that were placed in cages.

Mom enjoyed going to the local movie theater when she was young. On one occasion, Mom and her younger brother Jack went to a matinee movie and were the only people in the theater. The theater owners refused to show the movie and refunded their ticket money. Mom was so disappointed.

Occasionally, Mom told me stories about the struggles and challenges she faced growing up in a poor family. She emphasized how important it was not to waste food. She remembers her father going out into the woods to hunt rabbits and squirrels to bring meat to the table.

Mom graduated from Rhea County High School in Dayton, Tennessee, in the spring of 1948. While attending classes at the University of Tennessee, she trained to become a file clerk at the Federal Bureau of Investigation in Washington, DC. She then transferred to Knoxville, Tennessee, where she began working as a high-level security file clerk. After Mom and Dad were married, they were both transferred to New York City, where she continued working as a high-level security file clerk.

Lois Ouellette
Rhea County HS 1948

Mom resigned from the FBI on January 17, 1955. In her resignation letter to J. Edgar Hoover, she emphasized that "the reason for my resignation at this time is due to pregnancy," and "I want to thank you for the opportunity of having been employed by the FBI and to wish you and your associates continued success in all of your undertakings."

Lois at Graduation 1948
3rd from L

She later received a letter from J. Edgar Hoover dated January 24, 1955, concluding with, "It is a pleasure to know you have enjoyed your association with the Bureau and I want to take this opportunity to thank you for the kind remarks contained in your letter." My mother told me, on more than one occasion, that she did not care much for Mr. Hoover and was not happy with the fact that she was "forced" to resign from the FBI because she became pregnant.

Following resigning from the FBI, Mom moved on to her next career—the mother of seven children, where she focused her time and energy on the family.

Lois Ouellette

Mom later went back to work part time after Richard entered elementary school. She worked as the secretary for the Work-Study Program at Grafton High School in Grafton, Massachusetts, from 1975 to 1978.

During these four years, Jim, Paul, Marie and I attended Grafton High School while she was working in the office area alongside other school administrators and guidance counselors. It was fun stopping in and saying hello to Mom while at school. Every so often, I ran down to Mom's office to ask for a pass if I was late for class. I'm sure my teachers at the high school disapproved of my actions. Everyone at Grafton High School, even those who were not enrolled in the after-school job program, loved our mother.

Mom was a talented guitar and piano player. Her love of music and her musical talent were influential. John Jr. played the guitar. Jim writes music and performs vocals. I can play rhythm guitar, piano, perform vocals and write music. Marie plays the guitar and the piano and has an amazing voice. Neal plays drums, guitar, sings and writes music. Richard became our dedicated roadie, available to help with backup vocals and transport equipment. I am certain that my mother's musical inspiration led to the formation of our family band, *Slant 6 and the Jumpstarts,* in 1979.

Mom enjoyed typing and sewing. Anytime someone in our family needed a document or report typed, she was available to help. Her ability to sew and repair ripped clothing saved our family plenty of money over the years. She liked to create and design pillowcases and cloth towels.

Mom always wanted to have a driver's license and her own car. In 1969, she passed the Ohio Learner's Permit Test, and Dad bought her a 1960 American Rambler Ambassador. I will never forget the day in 1969 when she started the Rambler and accidentally put the car in reverse and backed it into the barn doors. She was shocked and surprised at what had happened, yet she quietly got out of the car, walked back into the house and started playing the piano.

I remember feeling so sad for her and going back in the house with her and listening to her play. Mom never ended up getting her driver's license but was happy that Dad supported her dream to own and drive a car. Fortunately, as we grew older and got driver's licenses, Mom had plenty of "chauffeurs" to drive her anywhere she wanted.

One of my favorite stories relating to both my parents took place while living in Grafton, Massachusetts, during the late 1970s. It became a ritual every Saturday morning when Dad would drive Mom to Super Stop & Shop in Westborough, Massachusetts. Dad dropped Mom off at the store and then ran a few errands. After completing his errands, Dad then drove back to Stop & Shop and sat outside waiting for Mom to come out with her groceries. As soon as Dad spotted Mom coming out the exit doors, he pulled up in front of the store and loaded the groceries.

On one special occasion, Dad was sitting outside of Stop & Shop waiting when Mom came out of the store waving a scratch ticket and shouting, "John! John! I won! I won!" Mom had bought a scratch ticket and won $10,000. This could not have come at a better time as inflation was at an all-time high and supporting seven kids, some in college, was challenging. This was one reason Dad came out of retirement in 1978 and went to work for Raytheon as a security specialist.

Ironically, the incident happened again the next week. Dad was waiting outside of Stop & Shop, and again Mom came out shouting, "I won again! I won again!" Mom had won $20,000 on a scratch ticket.

I never learned about these winnings until I received $500.00 in my stocking that Christmas. This was a significant amount of money and, knowing how tight the household budget was, I tried to give the money back to my mother a few days later when we were sitting alone in the dining room. This was when she explained to me what had happened at Stop & Shop. Our parents were able to use a portion of this money to pay off the mortgage on our house.

Mom mastered the art of cooking for a large family. She cooked enough for the entire family and extra portions for any friends or relatives that might stop by to visit. Dinners were normally around 6:30 to 7:30 p.m. Some of the more popular dinners Mom would cook included pot roast, chicken and dumplings, goulash, salmon, and peas, fried chicken with okra and corn bread, steak with baked potato and green beans, franks and beans, with brown bread, pork chops with applesauce, ham with boiled potatoes and carrots, to name a few. On Thanksgiving, Christmas, and New Year's, Mom would make turkey with meat stuffing, mashed potatoes, green beans, and cranberry sauce.

If an FBI investigation ever kept Dad out later than 8:00 p.m., which was rare, he called Mom and let her know he would be late. Dad would enjoy his dinner later in the evening. On the rare occasions when Dad arrived home around 10:00 or 11:00 p.m., Mom would make him a full breakfast of scrambled eggs, sausage, bacon, and toast.

Sunday breakfast was a tradition I regularly enjoyed before or after church. The time we ate breakfast depended on what time we went to church. We usually went to the 9:00 a.m. Mass. Sunday breakfast typically consisted of scrambled eggs, sausage, bacon, toast, and occasionally pancakes.

Mom and Dad attended as many of our school and sports events as possible. We all know the old saying, "You can only be in one place at a time." As I think back, I remember seeing my mother or father present at my school and sports events. As a retired teacher of thirty years, I remember meeting many parents with only two children and listening to them talk about how hard it was to attend their children's activities. *Imagine having seven kids*, I would think to myself.

Mom always welcomed our friends and neighbors into our home. There was invariably some kind of food being kept warm on the stovetop available to anyone who was visiting. Mom would offer to "fix a plate" for anyone that was hungry. Some of these available-anytime dishes included, southern style pinto beans and cornbread, fried pinto bean pancakes, chicken and dumplings, fried chicken, fried chicken livers, fried okra, and anything else that might have been left over from the previous night's dinner. There were many times when our friends, who showed up at our house even if they knew we were not home, just to hang out with our mother and have a "plate."

Everyone loved our mother and treated her with the greatest respect. If one of our friends was having family problems, she offered our house as a place to stay. Mom never went to bed until all the children who were still living at home were in for the night. I was fortunate to have been allowed to live at home during undergraduate and graduate school. I helped around the house and was sure to let my mother know if I was not coming home that night.

In the early 1980s, Mom went to work part time for Adele Maroney, a popular lawyer in the town of Grafton. They became good friends.

Mom worked part time for IMCO in South Grafton, an injection molding company, in the late 1970s. Ironically, both John Jr. and Jim worked at IMCO at some point, but never at the same time. Interestingly, while working at IMCO, Mom ran a machine that made Avon bottle lids and caps. She was a dedicated Avon products fan, and some bottles she bought from the Avon Lady had lids that she may have made.

During the early 1980s, Mom worked part time at the Electric Company in Westborough, Massachusetts. I remember driving her back and forth to work while attending Worcester State College. In the fall of 1980, she helped me land a part-time job as a cleaner at the electric company. I worked Friday nights from 5:00 p.m. to 9:00 p.m. I tried to avoid working during the week so I could focus on my studies.

Our mother always put family first. I have no doubt that raising seven children, along with many years of cigarette smoking, put a strain on her physical health. It was around the age of ten when I realized how much work it was for Mom to maintain a household of seven kids while Dad was at work. I began helping around the house with the cleaning, putting things away, and doing some of the yard work.

I continued to do what I could through the years to help my mom. She passed on July 20, 1995, at St. Vincent Hospital in Worcester, Massachusetts. How lucky we were to have had such an amazing mother.

CHAPTER 3

Knoxville, Tennessee
John & Lois

Our parents, John and Lois, met at the FBI Headquarters in Knoxville, Tennessee, in 1953. Mom had transferred from the Washington, DC headquarters, where she started her FBI career training, to become a high-level security file clerk. She was then transferred to the Knoxville, Tennessee office around the same time Dad was transferred from the FBI Headquarters in Detroit, Michigan, to the Knoxville Office. This is where they met and dated until their marriage on June 20, 1954.

Mom and Dad occasionally shared stories about their dating experiences. Like most dating couples today, they occasionally went out to dinner or to the movie theater together. They liked to go out on group dates with other FBI agents and their girlfriends. On some of these group dates, Dad and Mom would go with other agents and their girlfriends to a quiet location in the outer hills of Knoxville for a picnic lunch and target

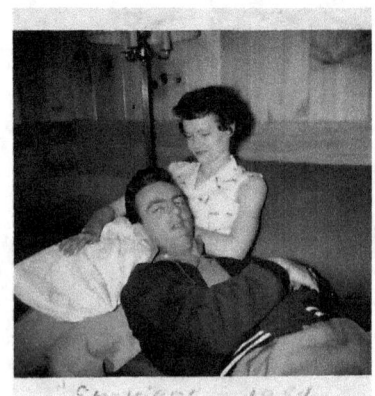

John Sr. & Lois

shooting. Hoover did not allow women to become FBI agents but encouraged female FBI office personnel to become familiar with firearms.

Mom, along with the girlfriends of other agents from the Knoxville Office, teamed up and planned the picnic lunches. These lunches often included fried chicken, gravy, and biscuits, along with fresh fruit or a home-baked pie.

Mom and Dad enjoyed attending FBI-sponsored office parties. They often went to house parties held by other agents and their wives or girlfriends. They played records, board games, and danced at these gatherings.

While our parents were stationed in Knoxville, the FBI was dealing with issues relating to the Ku Klux Klan, fugitives, bank robberies, and bootleging. Knoxville was known to be a part of the infamous "Thunder Road," which was a system of roads often used by bootleggers to transport moonshine throughout the region. There were also smugglers transporting whiskey from Kentucky to Tennessee to avoid state sales tax.

"Thunder Road" was the code name used by the FBI and other law enforcement agencies regarding the pursuit of bootleggers and smugglers crossing state lines. On many occasions, Dad was involved in the pursuit of some of these bootleggers while stationed in Knoxville. Hollywood took advantage of the folklore and legends surrounding the infamous "Thunder Road" by releasing a movie titled *Thunder Road*, starring Robert Mitchum in 1958. There was also a popular song being played on the radio at the same time titled *The Ballad of Thunder Road*, performed and co-written by Robert Mitchum.

Dad once told me about how he was involved in many of the roadblocks set up by federal law enforcement officials, hoping to capture these smugglers and bootleggers. He pointed out that there were many unpaved and unmapped side roads in the region, which made it difficult for the FBI and other law enforcement officials to determine the best times and locations to set up roadblocks.

He told me that in the movie *Thunder Road*, he would have been one of the agents at the final roadblock on Kingston Pike, where the infamous smuggler "Tweedle-o-twill" crashed his car while attempting to get around the roadblock. It must have been awkward when my parents discovered that one of my mom's uncles had a still out in the woods near my great-grandmother's log cabin in the late 1960s.

In the summer of 1969, while visiting our grandmother in Dayton and Mom's sister Clarice and family in Chattanooga, we took a day trip to visit great-grandmother Nora. I was so surprised to discover that she had an outhouse and an outdoor water well that required cranking a lever to bring the bucket of water to the top of the well. I remember sitting with Mom and Dad along with Paul, Marie, Neal and Richard in front of great-grandma's cabin when Uncle Buel offered to take John Jr. and Jim for a walk down a trail in the woods that surrounded her cabin.

When they returned from their short hike, John Jr. and Jim excitedly began telling us about Uncle Buel's moonshine still. Dad was so angry he told us to get in the station wagon, and he pealed out as fast as possible. I could hear Buel shouting, "John! John! Come back!" as I turned my head and watched him chase us. I never saw Buel again.

While stationed in Knoxville, Dad and another FBI agent had a warrant to arrest a draft dodger who had gone into hiding to avoid military service during the Korean War. When they arrived at the rustic mountain house, a woman greeted them and allowed Dad and the other agent to come inside and look around.

As mentioned, there was a warrant for this man's arrest, so the woman had no choice. While she claimed there was no one else in the house, Dad and the other agent heard someone walking back and forth in the attic space above. Dad shouted upward toward the ceiling and announced that they were FBI agents and had a warrant for his arrest. There was no reply from the person above, but they still heard someone walking back and forth. After locating the small entryway to the attic, they discovered that the only way to access the attic space was to climb up a ladder and poke their heads into the opening, leaving themselves defenseless as they pulled themselves upward through the small entryway.

Dad decided they would attempt to scare the person into surrendering himself and exiting the attic on his own. After it was determined that the person had walked to the far end of one side of the attic, Dad fired a shot through the ceiling at the opposite end of the attic. After firing the shot, he shouted, "The next one might not miss!" Suddenly the man shouted, "Don't shoot! I'm coming down! Don't shoot!" The man quickly descended from the attic, and they arrested him and took him to FBI Headquarters in Knoxville for processing.

John & Lois Cutting Wedding Cake

John Sr. & Lois
June 20, 1954 Wedding

Our parents were married on June 20, 1954. A few weeks prior to the marriage ceremony, Mom, a Southern Baptist, converted to the Catholic Church. After the marriage ceremony, they traveled to Washington, DC, and New York City and then made their way to Worcester, Massachusetts. While in Worcester, they visited Dad's family and took day trips to Cape Cod and Rhode Island beaches. Soon after returning home from their honeymoon, they were both transferred to the FBI Headquarters in New York City. Because of strategic planning by J. Edgar Hoover, they moved into an apartment right next to Paul Newman and his first wife, Jackie Witte.

John Sr. and Lois Honeymoon in NYC
June 1954

CHAPTER 4

The First Assignment:
Paul Newman (NYC)

John Sr. Ouellette Official FBI Photo

Soon after Dad and Mom were married, they were both transferred to the New York City FBI Headquarters. As directed by Mr. Hoover, they moved into an apartment right next to Paul Newman and his first wife, Jackie Witte.

This was a perfect opportunity for Mr. Hoover to have an FBI agent living right next door to a suspected communist sympathizer. It allowed the FBI to keep a watchful eye on the Newmans and any Communist-related anti-American activities they might be involved with. Mom was still working for the FBI as a high-level security file clerk, which allowed our parents the chance to present themselves as a newly married couple just starting out in life.

It is interesting to point out that during this post-WWII and Korean War era, America was focused on stopping the spread of communism here in the United States and around the world. This was a time often referred to by historians as the Cold War era. The term Cold War is often used to describe the political hostility between the United States and Russia between 1945 and 1990.

THE FIRST ASSIGNMENT: PAUL NEWMAN (NYC)

It was during this period that the FBI focused much of its time tracking Russian spies and identifying Communist sympathizers. McCarthyism was also prevalent in American society. McCarthyism refers to the campaign led by Senator Joseph McCarthy between 1950 and 1954, seeking out and accusing government officials and members of American institutions of being affiliated with the Communist Party. Many of these people were blacklisted or lost their jobs. It was later learned that most of these people were innocent.

Dad and Mom attended occasional cocktail parties hosted by the Newmans and had a great time. Dad told me that the Newmans served a variety of different cocktails and played records for their guests. He described them as being "down to earth," nice people who were concerned with social issues of the day and finding ways they might help children in need. Dad told me the Newmans were not communists.

I remember Dad commenting on how much he enjoyed movies that Paul Newman was involved with. He really liked the movies *Cool Hand Luke* and *Butch Cassidy and the Sundance Kid*.

I recall Dad taking John, Jim, Paul and me to see the movie *Butch Cassidy and the Sundance Kid* at the Avon Lake Theater when it first came out in 1969. It was fun watching Dad laugh at the part of the movie when the "Hole in the Wall Gang" stops the train, intending to steal money from a safe on board. Butch, played by Paul Newman, tries to convince Mr. Woodcock, the security guard, to open the train car door or they would use dynamite to blow it open. Mr. Woodcock refuses to open the door, and the train car and safe are blown to pieces. Butch, who is more concerned about Mr. Woodcock's safety, makes sure that he is okay before escaping the botched robbery. I had never seen Dad laugh so hard in a movie theater. Sorry, Mr. Hoover, Dad was a Paul Newman fan.

Dad smiled when telling the story about how he and another agent followed a suspected Russian spy in New York City, who ended up boarding the *Queen Mary* luxury ocean liner. Dad and his partner followed the Russian spy up the boarding ramp, staying about twenty feet behind while flashing their FBI credentials to boarding personnel.

After about an hour of watching the suspect from a distance, Dad realized the liner was pulling out of port. He quickly approached the captain of the ship and ordered him to return to the New York port so that he and the other agent could disembark the ship. The captain was not thrilled but had no choice. The suspect was able to stay on the ship, and no arrest was made. Dad laughed about the incident because the Queen Mary rarely ever returned to port after departure.

While living in New York City, Dad used to go for walks to the corner drugstore to buy cigarettes and sometimes came across some famous actors. He remembers having brief conversations with Basil Rathbone, "Sherlock Holmes," who was always out walking his dog. He would see Fred Gwynn, "Herman Munster" of the TV show *The Munsters,* walking around the park. This might explain why Dad enjoyed watching *Sherlock Holmes* movies and *The Munsters* television show. While in New York City, Mom gave birth to John Jr. I'll share more about the life of my siblings in later chapters.

CHAPTER 5

Kent State Shootings

On May 4, 1970, members of the Ohio National Guard, while dispersing a crowd of demonstrators at Kent State University in Kent, Ohio, opened fire, killing four students and wounding nine others. Dad was one of the lead special agents in charge of investigating this tragic event and the burning of the ROTC Building at Kent State University the night before.

Tensions on campus began on March 31, 1970, around noon, when President Nixon announced in a television broadcast that he had authorized US troops to invade Cambodia. Nixon's decision to invade Cambodia came when the US had already begun withdrawing American troops. This immediately sparked anti-war protests at colleges and universities around the country. The day after Nixon's speech, May 1, 1970, a protest occurred in the common area in the middle of the Kent State campus. According to Dad, many of these protesters were students and faculty along with other protesters who were not students at the University.

A second protest took place at the same location later that day, and that night, a crowd of intoxicated protesters gathered in downtown Kent. These protesters began breaking store windows and taunting the local police. The mayor of Kent, Leroy Satrom, declared a state of emergency.

The situation began to de-escalate, and most of the protesters left the area by 2:30 a.m.

On Saturday, May 2, Mayor Satrom asked the governor of Ohio, James Rhodes, to send in the Ohio National Guard. Upon their arrival at the campus, the Ohio National Guardsmen found that the ROTC building had been purposely set on fire. I will never forget that Saturday evening when Dad received a call from the FBI Headquarters in Cleveland and was instructed to head down to Kent State to investigate the situation. Dad was a supervisor of a squad and made a few quick phone calls.

Soon after, a car pulled up with a couple of the agents in his squad, and he was out the door and on his way. The FBI was called in because the ROTC building was a federal building. When Dad arrived, there was a crowd of at least 1,000 people surrounding the building and cheering. Some members of the crowd confronted members of the fire department to prevent them from doing their jobs. The National Guardsmen were able to disperse the crowd using tear gas, clearing the area by around midnight.

The FBI had already been aware that there was a house close to the Kent State campus, occupied by known communists who had been on the FBI's radar for a while. At about 1:00 a.m., Dad's squad went to this location, woke the occupants and had them line up and stand along the wall in the kitchen. After Dad and the other agents completed their search of the suspects and the house for weapons and explosives, they were told to remain in the area and not to leave the state. Dad, who was so offended by the smell of the suspects and how filthy the kitchen was, pointed to all the dirty dishes stacked in the sink. He asked a member of the commune, "Who does the cleaning around here?"

The suspect replied, "We don't clean! We are Communists."

Our dad came home late that night, or should I say early the next morning, and slept late. He did wake up in time to get us to the late-morning Mass.

On Sunday May 3rd, over 1,000 National Guardsmen arrived on campus, along with Governor Rhodes, who held a press conference. Governor Rhodes, along with Kent State administrators, announced that the protest scheduled for the next day, May 4, was canceled. This did not stop the protesters, who continued their confrontations with National Guardsmen.

On Monday, May 4, around noon, approximately 3,000 people, many of them onlookers, gathered at the campus Commons. At this point, the focus of the protests shifted from the Vietnam War to the National Guard and its occupation of Kent State. After demonstrators refused to back off, about 100 National Guard troops marched across the Commons, pushing the crowd up what is called "Blanket Hill" and down to the parking lot. Eventually, the National Guardsmen found themselves blocked by a fence and used tear gas while pointing their guns at the crowd. The protesters threw rocks and debris at the National Guardsmen, who began to retreat up Blanket Hill. Around 12:24 p.m., as soon as the guardsmen reached the top of the hill, they turned and fired their M1 rifles.

The guardsmen fired between sixty-one and sixty-seven shots over the course of about thirteen seconds. Some guardsmen aimed above the crowd while others aimed at them, resulting in four protesters being killed and others being injured. Dad was sent back down to the university after this tragic event to conduct a full investigation and interview witnesses.

Following the tragedy, a nationwide student strike took place at hundreds of high schools, colleges, and universities around the country. Dad continued his involvement with the investigation even after his transfer to the FBI Headquarters in Washington, DC, and then to Boston, Massachusetts. Dad was intrigued that little was written or said about the influence and impact of self-identified communists and anarchists, who were not enrolled as students, and were involved in the Kent State protests and other college protests around the country. While being an FBI agent had its difficult moments like Kent State, it also had positive advantages, which we'll explore in the next chapter.

CHAPTER 6

The Power of the Badge

We were fortunate to have FBI parents and could go places and see things that most people could not. This was because Dad carried an FBI badge.

My earliest memory of Dad using his badge to access a high-security area was when we were vacationing on Cape Cod one summer in the early 1960s. We visited the Army & Navy Store on Main Street in Hyannis and then drove down the road leading to the Kennedy Compound. Dad wanted to show us the location where the Kennedy family spent summer vacations. I remember traveling down the road a short distance and coming to a roadblock with a guard diverting people down a side street, preventing them from driving by the main entrance of the complex.

Upon our arrival at the checkpoint, the security guard politely told Dad that President Kennedy and most of the Kennedy family were at the complex and no one was allowed to drive by the main entrance. Dad pulled out his badge and showed it to the guard, who almost immediately replied, "Okay, Agent Ouellette," and instructed us to please not stop or get out of the car. I had to be four or five years old and remember thinking to myself how cool it was being allowed to travel down a road where no one else was allowed to go. It was my first realization that Dad had an important job and was well respected as an FBI agent.

Dad was fortunate to have four weeks of vacation every year. We enjoyed spending two vacation weeks visiting Dad's family in Massachusetts and two weeks in Tennessee to spend time with Mom's family. Our trips to Tennessee often included going to fireworks stores and celebrating my sister Marie's birthday.

It was while traveling from Ohio through Kentucky to Tennessee during one of these vacations that Dad wanted to show us Fort Knox. As many are aware, nobody enters Fort Knox. We arrived at the gate, and the security guard came out and told us he was sorry, but under no circumstances could we go any further beyond the first checkpoint. Dad took out his badge and showed it to the guard. We were told we could drive up to the second checkpoint to get a closer look at the building.

Upon arriving at the second checkpoint, we pulled over and could see Fort Knox in the far distance. Dad did not ask the security guard to allow us to proceed any further. I remember thinking how cool it was that we were able to get that close to Fort Knox. Dad had taken us to the theater to see the James Bond movie *Goldfinger* a few months prior to this trip. I have no doubt that this was part of the motivation to see Fort Knox. I remember how excited my brother John was during this experience.

Sometimes Dad took us to the FBI Headquarters in Cleveland on a Saturday afternoon. He gave us a private tour of the facility and allowed us to go inside the FBI gun vault. We were allowed to hold some of the guns while under his supervision.

I found the fingerprinting technology of the day intriguing and remember Dad telling us that sometimes criminals tried to burn off their fingerprints. The evidence room was another favorite of mine, filled with intriguing pieces of evidence.

In July 1968, we were on a family trip to Tennessee, and our parents took us on a secondary trip to the Cocoa Beach area in Florida. We stayed at a Holiday Inn not far from NASA. While on this trip, Dad took some of us there. NASA was closed to the public at the time, so Dad pulled out his badge and we were then granted access. Once inside, someone who personally knew Dad greeted us and brought us to the Apollo 11 rocket that was being built. The man told us, "This rocket is going to take the first men to the moon!"

I will never forget sitting down as a family in July 1969 and watching the Apollo 11 rocket launch. We were so excited and never missed the NASA updates presented by Walter Cronkite. It was beyond exciting to see Neil Armstrong set foot on the moon, live on television. That evening, after Armstrong had walked on the moon, our parents suggested we go outside and look at the moon and think about the fact that there were three brave American astronauts up there, two of them walking around the surface of the moon. I went back and forth from the live coverage on TV to our side yard and stared up at the moon.

Dad was able to get to know John Glenn, the American astronaut who was an Ohio native, quite well. They met while Mr. Glenn was visiting the Cleveland FBI Headquarters on business.

John Glenn was an American Marine Corps aviator, engineer, astronaut, businessman, politician, and the third American in space. He was also the first American to orbit the Earth, circling it three times in 1962. Following his retirement from NASA and the Marine Corps, he served as an Ohio senator. In 1998, he flew back into space aboard the Space Shuttle Discovery at age 77.

My father once shared a memorable story about a conversation he had with John Glenn at the Cleveland FBI Headquarters; John Glenn had surprisingly shared that, in his experience, being an astronaut was simpler than piloting an aircraft because, in his words, "NASA did all the work!"

FBI FAMILY STORY

In the late 1960s, Dad used his credentials to access NASA's Glenn Research Center in Cleveland and Sandusky, Ohio. Attending this Saturday trip were John Jr., my brother Jim and his friend Paul Neguluski. The NASA Glenn Research Facility has a 6,400-acre test area in Sandusky, Ohio, referred to as Plumb Brook, where ground tests are performed for the US and International Space and Aeronautics Communities. It was on this day that John Jr., Jim, and his friend Paul were allowed to experience the NASA wind tunnel. Imagine being allowed to play on such an expensive and sophisticated piece of multi-million-dollar equipment.

Other places one or more of us children were able to access with Dad include the Oak Ridge Research Facility in Oak Ridge, Tennessee, that was once the headquarters for the Manhattan Project, the Nike Missile Site W-64 in Lorton, Virginia, FBI Headquarters in Cleveland, Ohio, Washington DC, Boston, Massachusetts, and Knoxville, Tennessee, to name a few.

While it was fun seeing my father use his credentials to provide us with special access to places most people could not go, it's important to note that he never misused this power and our visits were always meant to foster family bonding and learning opportunities.

CHAPTER 7

The Valerian Trifa Case (Nazism)

J. Edgar Hoover insisted that there be at least one, preferably two agents, who could speak any existing foreign language for interrogation purposes. Dad was only one of perhaps two active FBI agents who learned to speak Romanian during his service in the FBI between 1957 and his retirement in 1977.

Dad attended the Defense Language Institute in Monterey, California in 1957, a US Department of Defense Institute now consisting of two separate entities, which provide linguistic and cultural instruction to the Department of Defense, the Federal Bureau of Investigation, CIA, and other federal agencies around the country.

While living in Cleveland and Avon Lake, Ohio, during the late 1950s and 1960s, Dad occasionally visited the Romanian Catholic Church in Cleveland to have conversations with the Romanian immigrants to support and maintain his Romanian speaking skills. These skills would come in to play in the late 1960s when members of the Romanian Community spoke out against Archbishop Valerian Trifa, who later became head of the Orthodox Episcopate, as being the leader of the Nazi Iron Guard in Romania during most of World War II.

Trifa was responsible for the murder of hundreds and perhaps thousands of Jews. Despite insufficient evidence to convict Trifa based on Romanian immigrants' accusations, he was finally brought to justice in 1982. The FBI was able to reveal his identity using new laser fingerprint technology and handwriting analysis on a postcard he had filled out forty years prior.

In 1982, Trifa was stripped of his US citizenship and ordered to leave the country. I remember Dad taking us to the Romanian Catholic Church in Cleveland and listening to him speak Romanian to various members of the church. Listening to those interactions with church members, I wondered what they were talking about, and I was impressed.

It was not until many years after Dad's retirement from the FBI that I learned he had been interviewing witnesses and collecting eyewitness testimonies from Romanian immigrants as evidence that would bring Trifa to justice. As I look back, I appreciate Dad's role in the investigation of Trifa and in bringing this evil man to justice.

CHAPTER 8

High-Profile People & Cases

Jane Fonda

In early November 1970, our family received exciting news: Dad was being promoted to a high-level position at the FBI Headquarters in Washington, DC, working directly under J. Edgar Hoover.

We moved to our new home in Lorton, Virginia, right outside of Washington, DC, during the Christmas break in December 1970. This was our last Christmas celebrated in Avon Lake, Ohio, and the first New Year's Day in Lorton, Virginia.

On November 3rd, 1970, Dad and his partner apprehended Miss Jane Fonda at Cleveland Hopkins International Airport upon her return from Canada. Miss Fonda was suspected of drug smuggling. The order for her arrest came directly from President Nixon. It was later learned that Nixon believed that her anti-Vietnam War protests could impact his re-election.

Following the arrest, Dad and his partner transported Miss Fonda to the Cuyahoga County Jail. It was at this location that Miss Fonda was able to slip out of one of her handcuffs and raise her "power to the people" fist right at the time the mug shot was taken. Dad was surprised that she could wiggle her hand out of the handcuff and admitted he purposely put the cuffs on loose because she seemed to be scared. Search "Jane Fonda mugshot" to see this famous photo.

As many are aware, this image became an iconic symbol of the feminist movement. Interestingly, Miss Fonda was still wearing the hairstyle she had during the filming of the movie Klute, a psychological crime thriller. Because of the mug shot, Miss Fonda's Klute hairstyle became one that many women around the country copied. Ironically, Dad was, in part, responsible for helping promote a new woman's hairstyle.

Soon after the arrest, President Nixon directed Hoover to drop the charges because he believed the arrest might increase her popularity. Dad and his partner returned to the Cleveland Cuyahoga County Jail to inform Miss Fonda that the FBI was dropping charges.

Upon arriving back at the jail, Miss Fonda was taken from her cell to a conference room where Dad told her, "On behalf of J Edgar Hoover and the FBI, all charges are dropped." Miss Fonda then turned to Dad and "flipped him the bird" and quietly walked out.

Dad enjoyed telling this story and chuckled at the "middle finger" incident. Ironically, Dad was a big fan of Henry Fonda, the father of Jane Fonda, and his performance in The Grapes of Wrath and how the movie portrayed the Great Depression.

The Beatles

Watching The Beatles perform on The Ed Sullivan Show on February 9, 1964, was the beginning of my lifelong commitment to being a Beatles fan. Ironically, the first song I ever heard on the radio that I liked was "A Hard Day's Night."

I liked the song "Yellow Submarine," released in 1968, and remember John and Jim playing the 45 RPM on their portable record player. I brought the "Yellow Submarine" 45 RPM to school and played it to the class as a part of "Show and Tell."

A popular time for us to listen to the radio was when we were traveling in the car. I remember John and Jim suggesting different radio stations to listen to while traveling around the Cleveland area. WKYC and WIXY 1260 were two popular radio stations we listened to regularly.

One of my fondest musical memories was when my brother John, on guitar, and our mother, on piano, played Hey Jude in the family room one August afternoon in 1968. Seeing Mom and John play together was fascinating and inspired me to learn how to play the guitar.

It was a few years before Dad passed when I asked him a question that had been on my mind for decades, "Were you ever involved with the investigation or surveillance of John Lennon back in the early to mid-1970s?"

President Nixon was afraid that John Lennon's anti-war songs could impact his re-election. Dad thought about it for a minute or two and replied, "We were keeping an eye on all the anti-war activists at the time." I expected such an answer as Dad knew I was a dedicated Beatle fan.

Dad did share with me that the Cleveland FBI Headquarters received an "alert" that the Beatles were performing in Cleveland on September 15, 1964, and "the FBI needed to be aware of the hypnotic influence the Beatles' music had on female listeners."

FBI FAMILY STORY

The following documents are declassified and available to the public.

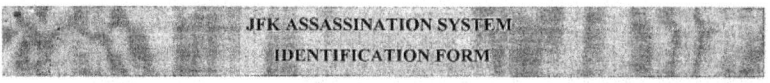

JFK ASSASSINATION SYSTEM
IDENTIFICATION FORM

AGENCY INFORMATION

AGENCY: FBI
RECORD_NUMBER: 124-10001-10256
RECORD_SERIES: DL
AGENCY FILE_NUMBER: 100-10461-492

DOCUMENT INFORMATION

ORIGINATOR: FBI
FROM: TWINER. GROVER C.
TO: DIRECTOR. FBI
TITLE:

Released under the John F. Kennedy Assassination Records Collection Act of 1992 (44 USC 2107 Note). Case#:NW 54463 Date: 10-12-2017

DATE: 12/01/1963

PAGES: 10

SUBJECT: SEE FBI 105-82555-951

DOCUMENT TYPE: PAPER. TEXTUAL DOCUMENT
ORIGINAL CLASSIFICATION: Secret   NEW CLASSIFICATION:

REVIEW DATE: 02/03/1997   UPDATE DATE: 11/03/2000

STATUS Redact

RESTRICTIONS:
JFK Act 6 (4)

COMMENTS:

FD-263 (Rev. 5-1-59)

FEDERAL BUREAU OF INVESTIGATION

REPORTING OFFICE	OFFICE OF ORIGIN	DATE	INVESTIGATIVE PERIOD
CLEVELAND	DALLAS	12/1/63	11/22 - 12/1/63

TITLE OF CASE	REPORT MADE BY		TYPED B
LEE HARVEY OSWALD ~~SECRET~~	SA GROVER C. TWINER	rmr	
	CHARACTER OF CASE		
	IS - R		

(JFK)

CLASSIFIED BY 5668SC0/6cc
DECLASSIFY ON: 25X (1)

3/5/97
10/22/96

REFERENCES

Bureau teletypes to all SACs, 11/22/63.
Bureau teletype to all SACs, 11/30/63.
Louisville teletype to Bureau, Cleveland and Dallas, 11/30/63.
Bureau teletype to all SACs, 11/23/63.
WFO teletype to Bureau, Dallas, New York and Pittsburgh, 11/23/63.
Cleveland teletype to Bureau, Dallas, New York, Pittsburgh and
    WFO, 11/23/63.

ALL INFORMATION CONTAINED
HEREIN IS UNCLASSIFIED EXCEPT   - P -
WHERE SHOWN OTHERWISE.   5-11-93
                                LEADS   Classified By 8568-CAD/gcl
                                             Declassify on: OUR RE:JFK
CLEVELAND:
                                             (5668 Sc0/ac; 3/5/96 JFK)
    AT CLEVELAND, OHIO

    Will continue efforts to locate the following:

APPROVED
COPIES MADE:
    5 - Bureau (RM)
    3 - Dallas   (RM)
    1 - Louisville (Info) (RM)
    3 - Cleveland (105-6774) 105-7674
        (1 - 62-1848)

SPECIAL AGENT IN CHARGE

DO NOT WRITE IN SPACES BELOW
100 -10 461 - 492

DEC - 3 1963
FBI - DALLAS

Dissemination Record of Attached Report					Notations
Agency					
Request Recd.					
Date Fwd.					
How Fwd.					
By					

~~SECRET~~

HW 54463 DocId:32113382 Page 2

CV 105-6774   ~~SECRET~~

IDENTITY OF SOURCE	DATE OF CONTACT	AGENT
CSCV-415-S CS DAVID LOWY	11/23/63 "	SA EDWARD P. GAZUR
CV-416-S (s) (x) (c&T(u)	11/23/63	SA JOHN N. OUELLETTE
JOHN J. SIBESIAN, Attorney, Cleveland	11/23/63	"
PETER LUCACI, Editor "American Rumanian News"	11/23/63	"
ANDREW HAMPU, Secretary General, Union and League of Rumanian Societies, Inc., Cleveland	11/23/63	"
CV-273-S	11/23/63	SA ARLO J. QUILL
CV-331-S	11/23/63	SA ROBERT S. BURGINS
CV-230-S	11/23,24/63	SA EDWIN B. BIRNEY
CV-297-S	11/22/63	SA MILTON P. MANDT
CV-463-S	11/24/63	SA ARLO J. QUILL
CV-399-S	11/23/63	SA ARLO J. QUILL
PCI JULIUS BENSON	11/22/63	SA EDWARD MC KASKEL
PCI FRANCISCO OCZIO	11/22/63	"
PCI WALLACE MOYER	11/23/63	SA JOHN J. KLISE
CV-445-C	11/23/63	"
PCI AL BAKER	11/22/63	SA ROBERT A. BILGREEN
CV-572-C	11/22/63	"

- C -
COVER PAGE

~~SECRET~~

John F. Kennedy

John F. Kennedy was assassinated on November 22, 1963, in Dallas, Texas. I remember attending kindergarten at Garfield Elementary School while my brothers, John and Jim, were students at St. Rose Elementary School. These schools were close to each other, and we could easily walk to and from school every day. This made it convenient for mom who needed to be at home caring for Paul and Marie.

I clearly remember the principal of my school, a nun, coming into our classroom and announcing that the president had been shot, and we were to go home and pray. As John, Jim and I walked home together, we watched people standing outside of stores that sold televisions and quietly watching the live news updates. Many stores that sold televisions placed TVs facing outward toward the sidewalk to entice people walking by to come inside and perhaps buy one. I remember a woman kneeling on the sidewalk crying as she grasped her rosary. This was normally a loud and busy street. I had never seen so many people silently staring at televisions and praying quietly. I am thankful that our mother forced us to sit in front of the TV and watch the president's funeral. We were not allowed to play or make any unnecessary noise. Ironically, Mom was born on November 22 and, because of this tragic event, she changed the date we celebrated her birthday.

In my adult years, I occasionally asked Dad about his role in the JFK assassination investigation. He was always hesitant to talk about this topic until a few years before his passing in 2015.

According to Dad, Lee Harvey Oswald had connections with a few suspected communist sympathizers in the Cleveland area. He interviewed these acquaintances and learned that there were others involved in some way, either directly or indirectly, with Oswald. He did not tell me their names. Dad told me that most likely there was a second gunman, and the "grassy knoll" theory is somewhat accurate. He pointed out that most likely Oswald and the second shooter were not aware of each other. Dad did not tell me the name of the possible second shooter.

Dad was involved with the Jack Ruby investigation. Jack Ruby shot Oswald two days after being accused of killing President Kennedy. Ruby had connections with some of the "strippers" in the Cleveland area. Dad and another agent had to track down these dancers and conduct interviews. He made it clear to me he was not comfortable tracking down these "strippers" at the Cleveland nightclubs. I have no doubt this was in part because of his Catholic upbringing.

I was excited to hear about the thousands of documents related to JFK that have been declassified and released in 2025. These documents are interesting, and it may take years for all the existing documents to be made available to the public. To my knowledge, there has yet to be any declassified documents released to the public relating to a second shooter.

Martin Luther King

There were a few occasions, while sitting at the dinner table, when Dad made some interesting comments related to Dr. Martin Luther King. I remember one instance when our mother, who had seen some of the news reports relating to Dr. King's visit to Cleveland that day, asked him how things went earlier. I was sitting right next to Dad and heard him whisper to my mother, "Mr. King was not very cooperative, and it was difficult to keep him safe."

Dr. King came to speak in Cleveland twelve times between 1956 and 1967. Many years later, I asked Dad about his experiences with Dr. King. He told me that King was under surveillance for national security reasons but also under the protection of the FBI because of the many death threats placed on him. Sadly, Dr. King was assassinated on April 4, 1968, six days before his next appearance in Cleveland.

Robert Kennedy

On June 5, 1968, Robert F. Kennedy was shot by Sirhan Sirhan at the Ambassador Hotel in Los Angeles, California. I remember Dad saying goodbye to us before he left for the airport the next day. He told us he would be gone for a few days on FBI business.

Upon his return three days later, things were back to normal. We were getting excited about the coming summer vacation and going to Tennessee and Cape Cod. I am not sure where everyone else was, but I felt it was the perfect opportunity to sneak into my parent's bedroom and peek at the files left out on Dad's desk.

On his desk sat a three or four-inch binder with the word "Confidential" on the cover. I opened the binder and saw pictures of Robert Kennedy lying on the floor, bleeding. Initially, I was overwhelmed by the blood near his head, and then I instantly felt sorry for his children, who would miss out on having a father to do fun things with.

I closed the binder after viewing two or three of the photos and left the room. I never told Dad I had seen the photos, but asked him many years later if there were any interesting conspiracy theories related to the Bobby Kennedy assassination. He told me, "No conspiracies."

I remember being with Dad while living in Lorton, Virginia, in the early 1970s and driving by the house where Ethel Kennedy lived in Northern Virginia. Dad saw a woman working in her flower garden with some men in suits and ties watching over her. He pulled over in front of the house and told me to stay in the car.

Dad exited our station wagon and held up his FBI credentials while walking toward the men, who were Secret Service agents. After talking with the Secret Service agents, he walked over and began talking with the woman for about a minute or two. After returning to the car, we drove away. He told me it was Ethel Kennedy, and he wanted to see how she was doing.

Ted Kennedy

While stationed at the FBI Headquarters in Boston, Dad worked with Senator Ted Kennedy, providing additional security at his public speaking events. Prior to transferring to Boston, while living in Lorton, Virginia, Dad received a call from Hoover at around 2:00 a.m. informing him that Ted had gotten into an automobile accident a few miles north of our home on Ox Road.

Hoover asked Dad to try to get to him before local and state police arrived at the scene. Dad arrived at the scene before anybody else and brought him back to our house where he slept on the couch until around 5:00 a.m.. I remember waking up around that time and seeing Dad and Mom helping someone get into our station wagon. Dad then started pulling out of the driveway while my mother stood watching.

As I was getting ready for school later that morning, I asked Mom who the guy was getting in the car with Dad. Mom replied, "Just a friend that Dad was taking to work." It was many years later when I asked Dad about the incident. He told me it was Ted Kennedy. I guess we can accurately say that Ted Kennedy slept at our house.

Jim and I met Ted Kennedy and received his autograph in 1980 at the Mart parking lot in Grafton, Massachusetts, while he was campaigning. The only thing I could think about was the fact that this was the guy who had slept at our house and Dad had driven to work early that morning.

Logan Airport

During the 1970s, there were a few incidents at Logan Airport in Boston, Massachusetts, involving hijacked planes. Dad told me that there was one incident when an already hijacked plane landed at Logan to refuel. Dad, in conjunction with the Massachusetts State Police, put together a plan to surround the plane and be prepared to intervene with the hijackers if an opportunity were to arise. After the plane landed, FBI agents and state police got into position while the plane was refueling.

While the plane refueled, Dad noticed that one of the state police officers was not standing next to the left jet engine as planned but stood behind it. The jet engine, still running in neutral, was so loud that the officer could not hear his walkie-talkie while the operation coordinator was trying to tell him to move to the side of the engine. After the plane was partially fueled, the hijackers became nervous and took off.

The second the hijackers put the engines into motion, the state police officer was "blown" into the air and landed on the ground, removing all his clothes in the process. While the officer was not seriously injured, it was pretty embarrassing to be lying on the ground naked. Dad was able to convince the local news teams not to embarrass the officer by reporting the incident on the news. The press honored his request.

The Tall Ships and the Queen of England (1976)

One of Dad's last major assignments prior to his retirement in July 1977 was providing security to the "Tall Ships" visiting the port of Boston during the summer of 1976 as part of the United States Bicentennial Celebration. He was also in charge of security for Prince Philip and Queen Elizabeth, who visited and toured Boston on July 11, 1976, as part of this celebration.

What I remember most about these events was seeing Dad standing at different locations and being somewhere in the background while watching the event being covered in the news. Dad was so happy and proud of the security the FBI provided for these special events. There were some arrests made prior to the start of the Tall Ships event and the arrival of the Queen as well as a few assassination plots discovered and prevented by the FBI. When talking with Dad about these events many years later, he expressed how nervous he was and how gratifying it was to have been a part of the security keeping the Queen and the Tall Ships event safe.

CHAPTER 9

Serial Killers /
Shocking Incidents /
Ten Most Wanted

After graduating from Grafton High School in May 1977, I was preparing to enter a postgraduate year at Worcester Academy in Worcester, Massachusetts. It was during the summer of 1977 that the infamous serial killer David Berkowitz, the "Son of Sam," was arrested and made headline news.

David Berkowitz, also known as the ".44 caliber Killer," was charged with killing six people and wounding seven others. Even though Dad had already retired from the FBI on July 30th, I thought he might have somehow been involved with the Berkowitz case. Later that August, when Dad picked me up at football practice, I asked him whether he was part of the investigation. He told me he was not directly involved. Being on the topic of serial killers, I asked him if he had ever arrested a serial killer. He thought about it for a minute and then began telling me about a case that took place back in the late 1960s while stationed in Cleveland.

The FBI had received reports that there was a person whose parents had not been seen or heard from by other family members for a few weeks. Dad, along with another agent, went to the man's home to ask questions about the whereabouts of his parents. There were no warrants, and they were there just to ask a few questions. The man, who was polite and "seemed to be normal," invited them in, offering a seat in his living room and asking if they wanted coffee. Dad and his partner politely refused the coffee and preferred to remain standing. He then asked the man if he knew where his parents were, and the man immediately replied, "Oh! In the attic!" Dad asked if they could go up and speak with his parents. The man replied, "Sure, follow me!"

After climbing the third-floor staircase to the attic, the man brought them to a partially hidden secondary room at the side of the attic and pointed toward seven large chests lined up along the wall. Dad and his partner drew their 38 specials and told the man to lie on the floor and keep his hands clasped behind his head. While Dad's partner stood guard over the man lying on the floor, he went over and began opening the trunks one at a time, exposing seven mummified bodies. The man simply looked up with a smile, as though there was nothing wrong.

Dad then asked the man if he had killed his parents and the others. The man told him they were not dead. He explained that he had used ancient Egyptian mummification techniques to mummify their bodies. Therefore, their souls were still lingering inside their bodies.

It was learned later that two of the bodies were the man's parents and the other five were those of missing people who had disappeared in the Cleveland area over the past few years. Dad and his partner arrested the man and brought him to the FBI Headquarters for due process and further questioning.

The Refrigerator Incident

A "letter bomb" was a term used by law enforcement officials to describe the process of using the US Postal Service to mail packaged bombs with the intent of killing the recipient. These bombs were rigged to explode when a person opened the package.

During the late 1960s, there was a man who lived in the Cleveland area who received a letter bomb. He opened the package at the kitchen table, right in front of his refrigerator. The explosion pushed the man backward into the refrigerator with such force that he had to be pried out using tools, leaving a clear indentation outlining his body as he was holding up his arms during the explosion.

Dad brought his entire squad to investigate the incident. Unknown to my dad at the time, one agent in his squad thought it would be funny to have the refrigerator moved to the Cleveland FBI Headquarters coffee break room to use for storing food and lunches. Dad had no idea this agent had pulled this prank and when he found out, quickly had the refrigerator removed from the break room and placed in the Evidence Room. Unfortunately for the agent and his family, Hoover found out about the incident and transferred him to Butte, Montana. The FBI was eventually able to trace the mail bomb to its source and arrest the murderer.

High Rise Suicide

My brother Jim told me a story that Dad had shared with him while living in Grafton, Massachusetts. There was an incident in Cleveland during the 1960s, when a man was either pushed or jumped out of the window of a high-rise building near the FBI Headquarters. When the man hit a fire hydrant, it caused his body to explode.

Dad and his squad were called to the scene to investigate and pick up and bag the body parts. After conducting research, I was able to learn that the incident may have been related to the Cleveland mob scene, but there was not enough evidence to make a connection. The man's death was ruled a suicide.

FBI Ten Most Wanted List

The FBI Ten Most Wanted list began in March 1950, when a newspaper reporter asked the FBI for a list of names and descriptions of the worst criminals they would like to catch.

Every so often, Dad pointed out a Ten Most Wanted poster hanging on a wall at a post office or federal building we happened to be visiting. He also had copies and updated versions it on his desk at home.

You can still find these posters today at United States Post Offices, state police stations, and local police stations around the country. We might never know the exact number of Ten Most Wanted fugitives Dad captured or helped catch, but I think it is a great idea for a book, though it would require a review of thousands of declassified FBI documents.

Dad did tell me about a Ten Most Wanted arrest he was involved with while stationed in Cleveland during the early 1960s. Herbert Hoover Huffman, who killed his wife on December 19th, 1960, in Cleveland, was the 144th person to be placed on the FBI Ten Most Wanted list.

On December 29, 1960, one of his fellow workers who saw his picture on the poster identified Huffman. It was Dad who answered the phone at the Cleveland FBI office when the witness called. After hanging up the phone with the informant, Dad, along with other available agents, went to the suspect's location and arrested him.

CHAPTER 10

UFOs

J. Edgar Hoover did not want the FBI involved in investigating unidentified flying objects. The Cold War, the threat of Communism, and apprehending foreign spies were at the top of his list of priorities.

There were two topics I liked to bring up when sitting with Dad with little or no distraction: the John F. Kennedy assassination and UFOs. My first encounter with FBI documentation relating to UFOs came about on a Saturday morning sometime in 1967. Dad was out doing errands while Mom was downstairs in the family room taking care of Paul, Marie, and Neal. John and Jim were outside playing somewhere, making it the perfect opportunity to sneak into my parents' bedroom and look at the files Dad brought home to review over the weekend.

UFO

I was nine years old and wanted to learn as much as possible about his FBI experiences. I remember opening a three- or four-inch-thick binder and seeing photos of what appeared to be pieces of metal and scattered body parts. The body parts were not human. I will never forget the photo of the head of this "being" with its "large eyes" and "small mouth." There was no nose, but two small holes where you would expect to find a human nose. My first thought was, *how sad it must be for the family of this being.* Then I thought, *would they know what had happened to him?*

UFO Zanesville, OH, 1966

Later that evening, while eating dinner, beans and franks with brown bread, I gave myself away. "Are UFOs real?" I asked Dad. I realized I had just confessed to sneaking around his desk and looking at his files. Sitting quietly, I waited to be scolded when, after a few seconds, he replied calmly, "There are many planets out there similar to ours that have intelligent life." I was so relieved that I did not get in trouble and learned that I must be more careful when looking at the files on his desk.

In November 1966, Ralph Ditter of Zanesville, Ohio, took a photo of a UFO hovering above his house. He placed the photo in the window of his barbershop to attract public interest. After learning about the photo, Dad and another agent were sent to Zanesville to interview Mr. Ditter. Dad learned that agents from Project Blue Book had already visited Mr. Ditter. They were frustrated that he had publicly displayed the photo at his shop and wanted the negatives of the photos. Mr. Ditter refused to comply and would not even give my dad the negatives.

My favorite UFO story Dad shared with me was an event that took place on the shores of Lake Erie in Cleveland, Ohio, in 1968. From time to time, the FBI was inadvertently drawn into UFO investigations, especially if there were concerns about national security or Russian technological advancements.

FBI agents worked in pairs. Dad and his partner responded to a call from a man who lived in a townhouse right on the shores of Lake Erie. Upon arrival, they were greeted and offered a seat in front of a spacious picture window that provided a view of the lake. The man then described how every so often, two or three huge metallic disks would fly in and out of the lake. He said that he never had enough time to grab his camera and take pictures.

While Dad took notes, the man calmly said, "Here they come!" At that moment, out of the water came three large, bright metallic disks that headed upward into the sky. After leaving the townhouse, Dad, who was the other agent's supervisor, told him, "We're not reporting this one!" The other agent replied, "Okay!"

Between 1947 and December 17, 1969, the US Air Force oversaw Project Blue Book, which was responsible for investigating UFO sightings. Project Blue Book Headquarters was at Wright-Patterson Air Force Base near Dayton, Ohio. The Air Force base is about a three-hour automobile ride from the FBI Headquarters in Cleveland. According to Dad, when Project Blue Book ended in 1969, a small crew was left intact and continued investigating certain UFO reports.

It was a few years before Dad passed when he told me about a UFO investigation that involved an object being followed by local law enforcement across state borders between Ohio and Pennsylvania. A few days after the event, he was sent down to Project Blue Book Headquarters at Wright-Patterson Air Force Base to interview three jet fighter pilots who were dispatched at around five in the morning, April 17, 1966, to pursue a UFO they picked up on radar. Dad liked to visit the air force base and had a few friends who worked there.

The incident began in Portage County, Ohio, when two deputies stopped to investigate an abandoned car. They saw a UFO hovering about forty feet above the ground, reported the incident, and tried to follow the UFO in their cruiser.

There were hundreds of eyewitnesses, including other police officers, and reports that three fighter jets were seen "attempting" to chase the UFO. Some witnesses also reported that the UFO "danced around and played with the fighter jets" until the object shot upward into the sky 86 miles away in Conway, Pennsylvania, leaving the fighter jets far behind. After meeting with Lieutenant Colonel Quintanilla, chief of Project Blue Book, a staff person escorted Dad to a conference room where he met the three pilots.

It is interesting to point out, Quintanilla had recently made a public statement that what the police officers and hundreds of witnesses had seen that morning was a satellite orbiting the earth. He then quickly revised his statement, saying that it was the planet Venus and there had not been any jet fighters dispatched in the area that morning.

Soon after arriving at the conference room, Quintanilla left to deal with some other business. He did not participate in the interview. When Dad asked the pilots what had happened and what they had seen, the first pilot who offered to speak replied, "I did not see anything!" The second pilot to speak replied, "I was not there!" and the third pilot looked at the other two pilots and asked, "Were we there or not?"

Dad laughed when telling this part of the story and understood why the pilots were hesitant to admit seeing a UFO and how it could jeopardize their flying careers. They quickly changed the topic and talked about the US Air Force.

The FBI also interviewed some of the civilian eyewitnesses as well as other police witnesses. Dad interviewed the two police officers who began the pursuit and Mantua, Ohio, Police Chief Gerald Buchert, who also followed the object and was able to take three pictures of it right before it zipped away.

I contacted Chief Buchert's son, Harry Buchert, while writing this book. Harry informed me that the pictures are still on file at the Mantua Police Station in Mantua, Ohio. This UFO incident, known as the "Great UFO Chase," inspired Steven Spielberg when filming the beginning of the movie *Close Encounters of the Third Kind*.

On Saturday mornings during the summer of 1974, I attended Sbrogna's Driving School classes on Grafton Street in Worcester, Massachusetts. After class, I often walked to a friend's house in Worcester to play basketball until my ride home arrived.

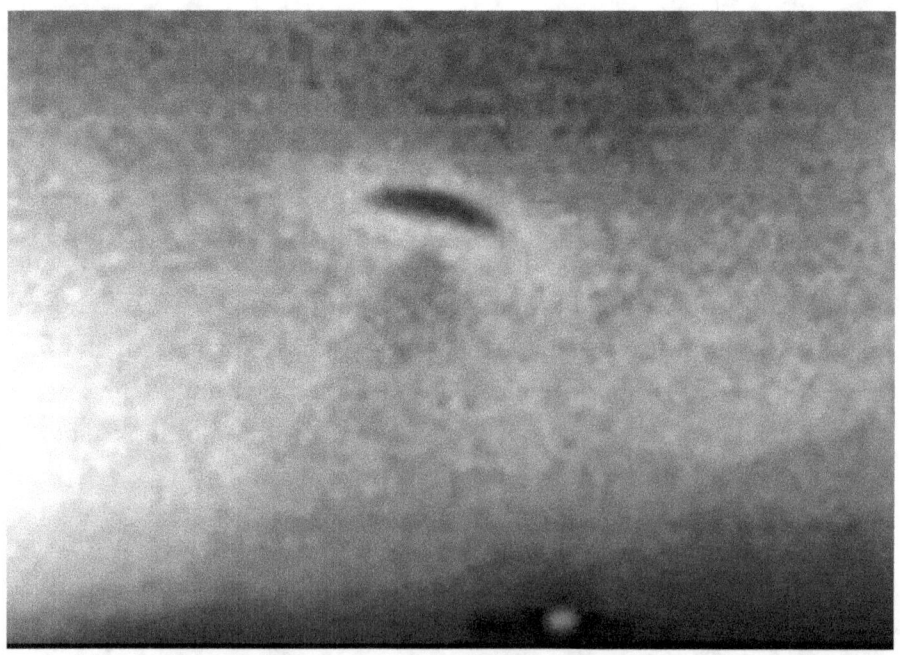

UFO Photo Taken by Mantua Police Chief Gerald Buchert - The Great Chase

One morning while playing basketball for about two hours, I realized no was coming to pick me up. I called home from my friend's house a few times, but no one answered the phone. I decided to hitchhike home, which was something I rarely ever did. I walked to the end of my friend's driveway and stuck out my thumb.

It only took about a minute or two when a woman in her late thirties or early forties pulled over and asked me where I was going. I answered, "Grafton Center." She told me to get in the car and that she was looking for a place in Grafton known as "Soap Hill." I told her I'd been there hunting a few times, and that it was also a popular "party" spot for high school kids. She asked if I had seen any strange flying objects in Grafton or in the area the previous night. I told her I didn't see anything, and when she stopped to let me out near my home, she gave me her business card, asking me to call if anyone from town had information. Her card identified her as being an agent with Project Blue Book. I had never heard of Project Blue Book until that day.

That evening at dinner, I told my parents that I was walking home from driver's education and a woman pulled over and offered me a ride. I did not mention the fact that I had been hitchhiking. I told my parents that she worked for a program called Project Blue Book and that there were reports of a UFO sighting in the Grafton Soap Hill area the night before. Dad asked me for her business card, and he took it to his office the following Monday to check it out.

While having dinner that Monday evening, Dad casually brought up the fact that this woman worked for Project Blue Book and was investigating UFO sightings in the area over the weekend. That would be the end of my story, but, years later, I learned about my brother Paul's experience that Friday night and my brother John's experience while working as a dispatcher at the Grafton Police Station that same weekend. Years later,

I found out about some interesting photos my brother John took that weekend of an unidentified flying object.

I spent many years as Paul's roommate at Virginia Circle during the early and mid-1970s. There were a few occasions when he told me about an event that took place one Friday night at Soap Hill. He never got far into the story without becoming upset and emotional. It was a while before Paul could tell me the whole story.

It was around 11:00 p.m. on a Friday night during the summer of 1974 when Paul and a few of his friends were sitting in a car and listening to music at Soap Hill when suddenly a huge machine with many different colored lights came down from above and paralyzed everyone in the car. Paul told me they could not move but saw a huge disk-shaped machine hovering over them. He described hearing a "pulsating humming" sound and then "everything went black."

A few hours later, they woke up lying on the ground outside of the car. He believes they were taken on board for a period and then released and left on the ground beside the car. My mother told me years later, when bringing up the discussion, that because Paul never came home that Friday night, Dad drove around town looking for him early that Saturday morning. This was why he never came to pick me up after driving school. I have no doubt that Paul's experience was real.

John, while working at the police station that weekend, received phone calls reporting UFO sightings. He did take a few interesting photos of an object in the sky from our front yard. Eventually, Paul came home later that Saturday and, as far as I know, never spoke about the incident until years later.

UFO Grafton, MA

One afternoon in the 1990s, I was living on North Street in Grafton Center and stopped by to visit Dad. We sat together watching the news on the small color TV he kept on the dining room table. There was a segment on the news relating to the possible existence of a place called Area 51, which some believed to be a place where UFO evidence is sent for analysis and research. This was a perfect opportunity to ask whether he had ever been there.

Dad told me he had never been to Area 51 but was present at a UFO crash site in central Ohio back in the 1960s where the FBI assisted other federal agencies with the task of "picking up UFO crash site evidence and loading it on trucks being sent to a facility in Nevada." He also told me that there was another occasion, while at Wright-Patterson Air Force Base, when an old friend took him on a tour of a building where UFO crash site evidence was being "re-constructed" by government scientists and engineers.

I wrapped up the conversation by asking him if he believed there was solid evidence of intelligent alien life existing on other planets? He avoided a direct answer by replying, "The universe is vast and endless. There must be other forms of intelligent life somewhere out there!"

It was in the fall of 1979 when my sister Marie and I were traveling on Rt.122 South in North Grafton. We were passing Grafton Pizza while approaching the intersection, where we could either take a left and drive by the Wonder Bar, known for great fish and chips, or bear right and head home. We both looked ahead toward the horizon, and both asked each other almost in unison, "What's that?" There was a massive yellow and green disk hovering westward over Westborough, Massachusetts. It had to be the length of five or six football fields, and we knew it was not the moon.

The moon was shining brightly to the left of the object. I remember the newly released George Harrison single "Blow Away" was being played on the radio at that moment. A few days later, a picture of this sighting was published in a local newspaper. There was a picture of an object someone had taken that evening, and it looked exactly like what we had seen that night.

One August summer weekend in 2012, I was with my wife, Mary, and daughter, Sarah, at the historic Portsmouth Inn in Portsmouth, New Hampshire. We, along with another couple and their daughter, had suites next to each other right on the water overlooking the pool and ocean.

That evening, while having a beer with Tony on the deck in front of our units, we saw three bright disks traveling across the horizon toward us that began accelerating at a speed unlike any we had ever witnessed. We shouted to our wives and kids, who were in the hotel rooms watching a movie, "Get out here! Get out here! You need to see this!" Tony then took out his cell phone and took three pictures of the objects. There was an article the following Monday in a New Hampshire newspaper describing the event, which included testimonies from some of the many witnesses in the area.

During the summer of 2024 while working on this book, I walked out to the front porch of my residence in York Harbor, Maine, to take a break. When I looked up into the sky over the ocean, I saw a bright metallic object darting back and forth at excessively high speeds and occasionally coming to a complete standstill. I videotaped the object before it disappeared after a bright flash of light. I posted the video on Facebook.

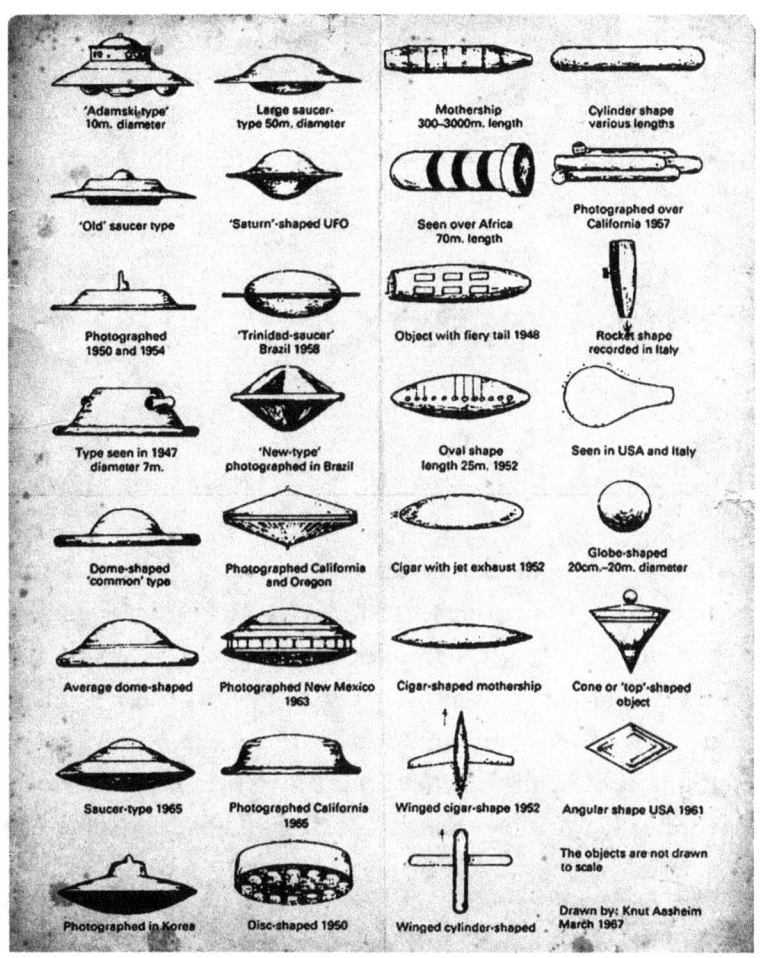

'Adamski-type'
10m. diameter

Large saucer-
type 50m. diameter

Mothership
300–3000m. length

Cylinder shape
various lengths

'Old' saucer type

'Saturn'-shaped UFO

Seen over Africa
70m. length

Photographed over
California 1957

Photographed
1950 and 1954

'Trinidad-saucer'
Brazil 1958

Object with fiery tail 1948

Rocket shape
recorded in Italy

Type seen in 1947
diameter 7m.

'New-type'
photographed in Brazil

Oval shape
length 25m. 1952

Seen in USA and Italy

Dome-shaped
'common' type

Photographed California
and Oregon

Cigar with jet exhaust 1952

Globe-shaped
20cm.–20m. diameter

Average dome-shaped

Photographed New Mexico
1963

Cigar-shaped mothership

Cone or 'top'-shaped
object

Saucer-type 1965

Photographed California
1965

Winged cigar-shape 1952

Angular shape USA 1961

The objects are not drawn
to scale

Photographed in Korea

Disc-shaped 1950

Winged cylinder-shaped

Drawn by: Knut Aasheim
March 1967

CHAPTER 11

Valentine's Day & Easter

Valentine's Day

Valentine's Day while in elementary school was a day when you were required to bring in a Valentine's card for every student in your classroom. My teachers would bring in cupcakes or cookies to be shared with the class. The best part of the day was having a short break from regular academics. These events were fun but made me nervous as I was pretty shy and found it difficult to believe that any girl in my class would give me a Valentine's Day card without also being told to do so by the teacher.

I remember every student had a small "mailbox" that we made and decorated in art class. During the celebration, we were told to walk around the classroom and distribute our Valentine's Day cards to each person's mailbox. This was challenging for me because I had to make sure that the male classmates received "cool" cards while the girls received more "romantic" style cards. After everyone finished delivering the cards, we returned to our seats to open our valentines.

Although I was not overly excited to take part in these Valentine's Day events, I learned how important it is to recognize the people you love and care about on Valentine's Day. Every year, I gave Mom a Valentine's card until her passing in 1995. I still send her a Valentine's card every year in the form of a prayer.

Easter

In the weeks leading up to Easter, we enjoyed Lent and having fish and chips on Fridays. Mom made us a delicious meal of either haddock and French fries or salmon and peas on toast. I remember the cost of fish and chips going from \$1.90 to \$2.05 during the late 1970s. Mom could not believe the price increase. I can't imagine what she'd think of today's prices!

During the late 1950s and 1960s while living in Cleveland and Avon Lake, Ohio, we celebrated Easter by attending Mass and recognizing the resurrection of Christ. I always enjoyed Palm Sunday the week before Easter and waving the palms we were given as we exited the church. On Easter Sunday, we would wake up early in the morning before church and search for our Easter baskets. Our baskets normally included a large chocolate bunny, marshmallows, pastel-colored crème and malted milk chocolate eggs along with foil-covered chocolate mini eggs and Brach's jellybeans.

Easter Mass was much longer than the regular weekly ones, and there was usually a strong incense being burnt. After church, we returned home and enjoyed scrambled eggs, sausage, bacon, toast and freshly squeezed orange juice. After breakfast, Dad conducted an Easter egg hunt for the youngest children while the older kids played in the yard.

We spent afternoons playing in the yard or watching classic movies such as The Robe, which debuted in 1953, The Ten Commandments starring Charlton Heston, released in 1956, and The Greatest Story Ever Told, which premiered in1965. Mom would make a ham with pineapple and cherries, boiled carrots and potatoes, green beans, and dinner rolls. Desserts normally included strawberry upside-down cake, coconut cake or perhaps a white cake with vanilla frosting decorated with jellybeans.

One of my most memorable Easter Sundays was when we were living in Lorton, Virginia. John, Jim, Paul, and I ran outside and played the basketball game known as HORSE during commercial breaks while watching the movie The Ten Commandments.

Easter Sundays during the 1970s while living in Grafton were fun. I enjoyed watching Neal and Rich enjoy their Easter baskets and having Easter egg hunts coordinated by Dad. I would go to Hebert's Candy Mansion in Shrewsbury, Massachusetts, and buy myself a one-pound chocolate bunny. Even as an adult, I have continued this tradition.

During the 1980s, I spent many Easter Sundays with my girlfriend and future wife Mary and her family. We continued to go to Mass at St. Philip's Parish in Grafton, Massachusetts. On some occasions, Mary's mom made a leg of lamb dinner, or we went to a restaurant for Easter brunch. Mary and I continued to visit the Hebert Candy Mansion in Shrewsbury, Massachusetts, to stock up on Easter candy.

While living in Whitinsville, Massachusetts, and then at 69 North Street in Grafton, Massachusetts, during the 1990s and 2000s, we hosted some of the Easter Sunday dinners at our home. After adopting Sarah, it was fun making her Easter baskets and having Easter egg hunts. I still enjoy celebrating Easter.

CHAPTER 12

Fall & Halloween

Dad loved the cool fall weather and beautiful foliage that came during the months of September and October. During the 1960s, Dad took John, Jim, Paul and me to a variety of different fun places on the weekends while Mom stayed home to care for our younger siblings. One of our favorite excursions was going to Huntington Beach Park in Cleveland, Ohio.

Huntington Beach Park was a place where we could go fishing, walk the trails, and enjoy the foliage. There were buckeyes everywhere, and when Dad was not looking, we would have "buckeye fights." I remember one occasion when Dad had us looking for leaves shaped like ghosts.

Sometimes while visiting Huntington Beach Park, we played "Mission Impossible," a game created by John and inspired by the TV show, *Mission Impossible*. The game was simple. John gave us about a minute or two to hide along the trails and then be hunted down by John and captured.

Fishing at the park was another activity we enjoyed. We caught carp, sheepshead, perch, and white bass. In most situations, we threw the carp and sheepshead back into the lake because we were under the impression that these were "bottom fish" and not the best to eat. Occasionally, other people fishing on the pier saw us working our way down to the edge of the pier to release the carp and sheepshead back into Lake Erie and asked if they could have them as it would be their dinner that evening. We gave these fish away to anyone who asked.

At Huntington Beach Park, small cliffs offered a daring challenge for children ages five through eight. These cliffs were not dangerous, but if you lost your balance, you would roll down and land on the soft beach sand.

To get from the top section of the park to the beach, people had to take a series of stairs with intermittent platforms. Some of these platforms had picnic benches and grills. I remember one occasion when John organized a game he called "conductor." This involved stopping at each platform along the staircase and pretending you were in a train caboose. Simple fun.

There was a park in or near Cleveland that we referred to as "Wiggly Hills." Kids brought pieces of cardboard to sit on to slide down the terraces as the grass was patted down and rather slippery. I was so excited when Dad informed us we were going to "Wiggly Hills" for a Saturday afternoon outing.

During the early 1960s, while living on 115th Street and Thoreau Road in Cleveland, we went to small family-owned stores to purchase Halloween costumes. These costumes came in a box with an open window so you could see the mask inside. The mask had a stretchy cord that kept it stable on your face while you wore it.

The most popular Halloween costumes of the 1960s were Superman, Rocky & Bullwinkle, Spiderman, The Beatles, Casper the Friendly Ghost and any of the classic Universal monsters such as Frankenstein, The Wolfman, The Mummy, Bride of Frankenstein, Phantom of the Opera, Creature from the Black Lagoon and the Invisible Man. Ghosts and witches were available in different styles. During the early 1960s, John was an astronaut, Jim a pirate, Paul the Wolfman, and I dressed as a knight in armor. There were a few occasions when Marie was a princess with a magic wand.

We would come home after trick-or-treating and sit on the living room floor. I remember dumping our bags of candy out on the carpet to access our "loot." We bartered and bargained with each other, exchanging candy as Mom watched, so we were fair and honest.

The more popular Halloween candy of the 1960s were Chocolate Hershey Bars, Butter Fingers, Babe Ruth Bars, Candy Corn, Milky Way Bars, Three Musketeers Bars, Clark Bars, Reese Cups, Good & Plenty, Dots, and Mallow Cups, to name a few.

Mueller's Licorice

I must have been four or five years old when I first went out trick-or-treating and remember dumping out my bag of candy and picking up a small box of Mueller's Space Age Licorice Cigarettes. After taking my first bite of this black licorice, I looked at my mother and asked, "What is this?" She told me it was licorice and that if I did not like it, I did not have to eat it. I loved it and still enjoy black licorice today.

I was so excited to see the premiere of the animated TV special, *It's the Great Pumpkin, Charlie Brown,* on Thursday night, October 27, 1966, four days before Halloween. As an eight-year-old Halloween enthusiast, this TV special changed my life forever. I continue to watch this classic Halloween special at least once, if not multiple times, every fall prior to Halloween.

During the mid to late 1960s, while living in Avon Lake, we were fortunate to have an old barn built as a small two-horse stable. This was a perfect location for telling ghost stories. After dinner during the month of October, Dad would take us out to the old barn carrying a carved pumpkin with a lit candle inside. He then told us a ghost story he made up and concluded by singing a rendition of *Ghost Riders in the Sky*. I do not remember any specific ghost stories but do recall that, while telling a story, he would include an occasional "Boo!"

Living in Cleveland and then on Moore Road in Avon Lake provided us with excellent neighborhoods for trick-or-treating. Many of the houses in Cleveland were old, historic houses, while the ones on the northern section of Moore Road were relatively new and close together. These homes were built after World War II, at the start of the baby

Halloween Haunted House

boom. There were a few occasions when our parents allowed us to have post trick-or-treat parties at our home or in the barn in Avon Lake. The parties held at our house in the dining room in 1967 and 1968 included a few of the neighbor kids. Mom made chocolate cupcakes with orange frosting while Dad played the *Chilling, Thrilling Sounds of the Haunted House* record released in the early 1960s. After the party, we sat at the dining room table and traded candy. Neal was too young to go trick-or-treating, and Richard was only about a month old.

During the 1960s, we enjoyed watching the legendary late-night host "Ghoulardi" who presented low-budget B movies while performing silly skits at breaks. While living in Virginia, we watched a show called *Sir Graves Ghastly,* who also hosted old monster and horror movies. Jim and I are still dedicated *Svenghoulie* fans and watch his show every Saturday night at 8:00 p.m. on Me-TV. Svenghouli and his side characters allow us to enjoy Halloween every Saturday night year round. I was fortunate to have appeared briefly on his show by submitting a short video on one of his "Spawn of Svenghoulie" segments in 2022.

**Paul Ouellette -
Ghoulardi Costume 1973**

It was a Friday night on Halloween in 1969 when we had a post trick-or-treat party in our old barn. I remember staying out and trick-or-treating with a neighbor until ten that evening, way past trick or treat hours. I was late for the Halloween party in the barn, but still happy that I made it back in time to enjoy some festivities. Dad was not thrilled that I had been gone for so long, so I shared my candy with my brothers and sister, thinking that it might somehow make up for my behavior.

I thought it was interesting to see the candy and candy wrappers all over the floors at school the week after Halloween. Everyone had candy in their pockets and lunch containers.

My last trick-or-treat took place when we lived in Lorton, Virginia. After moving to Grafton, Massachusetts, in 1972, while still in the seventh grade, my trick-or-treat days would end. I remember playing basketball at the outdoor basketball courts on North Street in 1972 and 1973 and watching the trick-or-treaters walking up and down North Street. At this time, Dad would take Marie, Neal, and Richard trick-or-treating up Worcester Street and North Street. Even though my trick-or-treating days had ended, I continued enjoying the fall season and the Halloween decorations put on display every September and October. It's still my favorite time of the year.

While in high school, Halloween became an opportunity to attend Halloween costume parties at someone's house when invited. If there were not a Halloween party to attend, I looked for a scary place to visit. One of these places was the old Grafton State Hospital in North Grafton. The

Grafton State Hospital closed in 1973 and was abandoned for about ten years.

The Grafton State Hospital was originally part of the Worcester Asylum in the late 1800s and was eventually taken over by the state and expanded to become the Grafton State Hospital. This was an experimental institution where patients were studied to better

Grafton State Hospital 1903

understand mental illness. We learned that electrical shock therapy, steam bath therapy, lobotomies, isolation therapy, and burial therapy took place at this facility. Many of the patients who had no family or friends to care for them were secretly buried around the old stone water tower with a simple stone with a number left as a marker.

There were a few Halloween evenings in the mid-1970s when my brother Jim and I, along with some of our friends would drive onto the old state hospital grounds and listen to the radio. There were a lot of strange things that happened while hanging out on the state hospital grounds. I later learned that some patients who were released from the institution when it closed in 1973 had returned and were living in some of the abandoned buildings or hiding in the tunnels that connected some buildings. These tunnels were built to keep patients out of sight while being taken from building to building. On one occasion, while we were hanging out at the state hospital, I looked up and saw a man with a long beard staring intently at us from one window of an abandoned building.

It was interesting to me that there were many old, abandoned houses in Grafton during the 1970s. After conducting some independent research while in college, I compared the population statistics of Grafton prior to 1973, before the state hospital closed, and the increase in population after it closed. In my opinion, people did not want to live in a town where dangerous and violent patients might escape and be a threat to the townspeople. The closing made people more comfortable moving to Grafton. Many older residents remember the town going into lockdown when dangerous patients escaped from the high-security lockup building.

I believe there was a stigma associated with living in Grafton when the state hospital was open. There were a few occasions while attending Grafton Middle School when people from surrounding towns saw my Grafton Indians shirt or jacket and asked me if I was a "looney." I would respond with a laugh, "Yes! I am coming to get you!"

A trip to Spider Gates, the old Quaker Cemetery in Leicester, Massachusetts, was regularly a conversation prior to Halloween while I was in high school. The cemetery was nicknamed "Spider Gates" because the entrance gates look like a spider web.

There was a documented murder case involving a young girl from Worcester, whose body was found at the cemetery in the 1920s and supposedly a suicide by hanging from the large tree next to the entrance gates. People claimed to see the ghost of a young girl walking the cemetery grounds and the image of a young man hanging from the tree.

I drove to Spider Gates with some high school friends a few days before Halloween Eve in 1976. We never exited the car and left after about a minute because it was so dark and eerie.

During the month of October while in high school, the Edgemere Drive-In Theater in Shrewsbury, Massachusetts, was a popular place to go on Friday and Saturday nights. I enjoyed seeing *Night of the Living Dead* and *The Texas Chainsaw Massacre* on multiple occasions at this venue. It was a great place to bring a date and attempt to scare them while enjoying popcorn and hush puppies.

I enjoyed my childhood Halloween experiences again through my daughter Sarah when taking her trick-or-treating in Grafton during the

2000s. Sarah impressed me when she and her friends continued trick-or-treating while in high school.

Halloween 2019 -
Stone House Bed & Breakfast
Chester, VT

Carol and I have celebrated a few Halloweens at the historic Mount Washington Hotel in Bretton Woods, New Hampshire. The hotel hosted a Halloween costume party in the "Cave" in the basement. This stone cave-like structure was used as a speakeasy during Prohibition.

While Sarah was attending Hobart and William Smith Colleges in Geneva, New York, we stayed at nearby Cobb Cabins. We would bring Halloween decorations and enjoy the festivities taking place in the area.

While living in Chester, Vermont, and operating the Stone House Bed and Breakfast & Kettle Corn Company between 2018 and September 2023, I decorated the house, drawing upon a colonial-style Halloween theme. These decorations included traditional witches, ghosts and scarecrows, along with pumpkins and cornstalks. We enjoyed watching the tourists pull over to the side of the road and take pictures.

More recently, we have celebrated Halloween by visiting Nantucket and taking a Ghost Tour, walking through the House of Frankenstein Wax Museum in Lake George, New York, spending the weekend in Gettysburg, Pennsylvania, and sitting at the Batson River Brewing Company in Kennebunkport, Maine, watching the trick or treaters going to the different businesses that were giving out candy.

In my opinion, Halloween season begins after Labor Day and ends on "All Souls Day," the day after Halloween.

Halloween - Stone House B&B

CHAPTER 13

Thanksgiving & Christmas

Thanksgiving

Thanksgivings during the late 1950s and 1960s were relaxing and enjoyable. We would draw a turkey based on the shape of our hand in first and second grade. The thumb served as the head, with the other fingers symbolizing the feathers. We colored these and printed the words Happy Thanksgiving somewhere at the bottom of the paper.

I remember asking my mother if I could help wash the turkey. I recall some of these turkeys weighing up to thirty pounds or more. It was fun watching the Macy's Thanksgiving Day parade on television and seeing the large floats. Our favorites were Rocky and Bullwinkle, Mickey Mouse, Donald Duck, Snoopy and Betty Boop, to name a few. Marie liked the Cinderella float. After moving to Avon Lake, Ohio, in 1965, we began to play touch football in our large backyard. These games could be rough at times when one of us tackled the ball carrier.

Mom made homemade giblet gravy to go with her turkey, mashed potatoes, meat stuffing, green beans, dinner rolls, and cranberry sauce. Not everyone liked giblet gravy, so Mom had a can of store-bought gravy available. I loved the giblet gravy. We spent Thanksgiving Day afternoons watching football and playing out in the yard.

While living in Lorton, Virginia, during the early 1970s, we continued to enjoy family Thanksgivings and playing touch football in our side yard. It was during the 1970s that The Macy's Day parade introduced the Sesame Street, Tom Turkey, Big Bird, Kermit the Frog, Bert, and Ernie and Animal House floats, to name a few.

Thanksgiving 1968 Marie Hiding Below at Bottom L - Lois, Aunt Edna, & Dad

After moving to Grafton, Massachusetts, in 1972, we continued to enjoy Thanksgiving as a family. We played touch football at the Norcross playground field on Worcester Street across from Virginia Circle. Many of our neighbors and friends joined in the fun. I enjoyed going hunting out in the woods behind our house early Thanksgiving morning and often came home with a few pheasants to cook along with the turkey.

It was while attending Grafton High School as a sophomore in the fall of 1974 that our football team played its first Thanksgiving Day football game. We played Bellingham High School and won twenty-two to zero. My brother, Jim, played defensive end and sacked the quarterback in what many considered to be the defensive play of the year.

The 1980s were a time when Thanksgiving evolved into a kind of reunion weekend. Mary and I were dating, and I spent part of Thanksgiving Day with her family. The Wednesday evening before Thanksgiving Day became an opportunity to go to The Old Post Office Pub in North Grafton and party with former high school friends and associates. We were pretty much free from the responsibility of preparing and cooking a large dinner. We would go to many of the Grafton High School Thanksgiving Day football games. These games became an opportunity for friends, family, and alumni to socialize with former high school friends and families.

During the 1980s and 1990s, our band, Slant 6 and the Jumpstarts, sometimes played live somewhere the Wednesday before Thanksgiving. I remember playing at Sir Morgan's Cove and The Blue Parrott in Worcester. We were asked to give out free frozen turkeys between songs while performing there. Mary and I participated in the Whitinsville 5-Mile Turkey Trot at 8 a.m. Thanksgiving morning.

The 1990s and 2000s became an era when different members of Mary's family hosted Thanksgiving at their homes. We had many nice Thanksgiving gatherings at our house on North Street. I enjoyed doing the preparation work on the Wednesday prior to Thanksgiving.

I currently enjoy Thanksgiving with Carol, and we keep the day simple and relaxing. I look forward to Thanksgiving; it is one of my favorite holidays.

Christmas

L – R John Jr. and Jim 1958

Christmas was a special time for our family. Even as we grew older, everyone seemed to find their way back to our parents' house at Virginia Circle in Grafton, Massachusetts, on Christmas Eve or Christmas Day. During the 1990s, we began a new tradition of gathering at our parents' house on Christmas Eve so we could spend Christmas Day with our families.

Christmas during the late 1950s and early 1960s began with going out and selecting a Christmas tree from a local vendor, usually a week or two before Christmas. Vendors often set up these Christmas tree lots next to a car dealership or on a small empty lot.

I remember living on 115th Street and Thoreau Road in Cleveland, where we could walk a short way up the street to pick out a fresh-cut Christmas tree. On one occasion, it was snowing, and Dad was able to drag the tree through the snow all the way back to our house. Setting up the tree in a stand and balancing it was constantly a challenge. Dad would carefully wrap the lights around the tree and place an angel or star at the top. These were old-fashioned lights that required every bulb to be working to maintain a connection with the other lights. Next, we carefully placed ornaments on the tree limbs and then tinsel. We children always put too much tinsel on the tree. I eventually figured out that our parents had removed the "globs" of tinsel and balanced the ornaments after we were asleep.

Christmas Eve was a quiet time spent sitting around the fireplace and listening to Christmas records or watching a Christmas special on TV. Dinners on Christmas Eve were usually simple, perhaps a Chef Boyardee pizza kit or TV dinners because Mom was busy doing preparations for Christmas dinner the next day.

As young children, we would lie in bed trying to stay awake, listening for Santa in his sleigh to land on our roof. During the late 1950s and early 1960s, we had a cardboard fireplace Dad set up because we did not have a real fireplace. Eventually, we had a real fireplace when we moved to Avon Lake, Ohio, in 1965.

Christmas Day began with opening gifts and looking to see what surprises we had in our stockings. We then prepared to go to Mass to celebrate the true meaning of Christmas—the birth of Christ. Our parents' nativity was a reminder of the true meaning of Christmas.

Staying up late attempting to wait for Santa's arrival made it challenging to get ready for Mass early the next morning. I also had to deal with the pain associated with wearing dress shoes that never fit. It was not until I was in middle school that a doctor informed me I had flat feet and problematic bunions. To make things worse, I also had a gag reflex issue, and wearing a tight tie made me gag. In short, dressing up for any occasion was and still is a physical nightmare. I avoid any events that include formal suits, tuxedos, and dress shoes. As I grew older, I was no longer required to wear a tie and formal hard-bottom dress shoes to church. I began to enjoy going to Mass.

After Mass, we returned home to enjoy an amazing breakfast of scrambled eggs, bacon, sausage, and toast with freshly squeezed orange juice. We continued to play with our new toys while Dad played Christmas records.

Later in the day, we gathered and enjoyed a fantastic Christmas dinner of turkey, meat stuffing, bread stuffing, homemade giblet gravy, mashed potatoes, green beans, dinner rolls, and cranberry sauce. We enjoyed the turkey dinner leftovers for the next few days after Christmas. The day after Christmas, Mom took a large portion of leftover turkey, added some of her homemade giblet gravy, and baked it in the oven.

As previously mentioned, Christmas dinner was amazing. Christmas desserts were also delicious. The desserts included chocolate pudding pie, pecan pie, homemade apple pie, and fruitcake. I love fruitcake!

After Christmas dinner, we watched one of the old black and white versions of *A Christmas Carol*. It was during the 1960s and 1970s that many of our favorite Christmas specials debuted on television for the first time. *Mr. Magoo's Christmas Carol* debuted on December 18, 1962. This was the first animated Christmas special to be produced for television. *Rudolph the Red-Nosed Reindeer* premiered on December 6, 1964, while *A Charlie Brown Christmas* debuted on December 5, 1965. The movie *It's a Wonderful Life* also became a Christmas seasonal favorite.

Mom loved going to Mass on Christmas Eve whenever possible. It was Christmas Eve, December 24, 1968, when Dad wanted to give Mom a break from wrapping presents and Christmas Day dinner preparations. He asked John to watch us for about five minutes and then dropped Mom off at church to attend the midnight mass. Dad quickly returned home, and before coming back inside, took a moment to enjoy a cigarette by the creek behind our apple orchard, to appreciate the peace and serenity. By this time, our oldest brother, John Jr., was certainly mature and responsible enough to keep an eye on us for short periods of time. Although nothing eventful happened that night, Dad often reminisced about this peaceful moment on Christmas Eve in 1968.

While living in Cleveland and Avon Lake, Dad took us downtown to see the department store Christmas window displays and decorations. These department stores included Halle's, Higbee's, May Company and Sterling-Lindner-Davis, to name a few. These excursions also included a visit with Santa and Mr. Jingleling.

Mr. Jingleling was an interesting holiday character created in 1956 by Frank Jacobi of Jacobi Advertising out of Chicago. Walter Halle, president of Halle's Department Store in Cleveland, asked Jacobi to create a new holiday character for the 1956 Christmas season. The store promoted Mr. Jingleling as the "Keeper of the Keys" to Toyland.

Mr. Jingleling became so popular the first year that he became an attraction in the Cleveland area for many more years to come. I felt he was scary and somewhat resembled a "devil." Google his name for pictures, and you will see why I thought this. While I kept my distance, I enjoyed seeing his commercials on TV as a reminder that Christmas was coming. Mr. Jingleling gave out cardboard keys for children to wear around their necks. While in Cleveland, we also visited the Cleveland Train Station Terminal Tower to see the enormous Christmas tree on display.

It is interesting how certain songs can bring back memories and help establish personal timelines. I remember hearing the song *Snoopy's Christmas* by *The Royal Guardsmen* on the radio during the 1967 Christmas season. Dad enjoyed listening to this holiday song and had a smile on his face whenever hearing it on the radio. He also liked *The Chipmunk Song (Christmas Don't Be Late)* first released in 1959, *Jingle Bells* by *The Singing Dogs* released in 1955, the *Christmas with Chet Atkins* album,1961, and *The Little Drummer Boy* by *Harry Simeone Chorale*, to name a few.

I remember some gifts that appeared under the Christmas tree in the early 1960s. I received a plastic castle with small plastic knights that I played with for hours at a time. Mr. Potato Head, Erector Sets, Slinky's, Universal Monster Model Kits, Footballs, Marbles, Chess & Checker games, Science Kits, Rocket Model Kits, Parcheesi, Candyland, Monopoly, and toy guns were just some gifts we received as young children. A few gifts I remember Marie receiving include dolls, drawing kits, Easy Bake Ovens, and Etch a Sketch, to name a few.

John, Jim, and Mark with Santa Mid 1960s -Mark is Wearing Mr. Jingling Key

While living in Cleveland, Ohio, Mass was spoken in Latin. I learned what to do during Mass by watching Dad. It was simple: I would stand, sit, kneel, make the sign of the cross, say amen, and go to communion when he did.

When we moved to Avon Lake in 1965, we attended St. Joseph's Church, where Masses were spoken in English. I remember how happy I was to understand what was being said.

As I grew older, I enjoyed watching Marie, Neal, and Richard open gifts. By the time I was in middle school, I received new clothes and perhaps a new record album for Christmas. I was thankful to be given new clothes, especially jeans and T-shirts. While in high school, I continued to enjoy the awesome Christmas dinners Mom made.

L – R Neal, Rich, Mark, Dog - Millie

New Year's Eve and New Year's Day were also an enjoyable time for our family throughout the late 1950s through the 1970s. It was a time to relax and watch football. Mom continued to cook large breakfasts in the morning and a turkey dinner later in the day.

Christmas 1970 and New Year's Day 1971 were interesting and memorable. This was when we transitioned from Avon Lake, Ohio, to Lorton, Virginia. Dad had been promoted and reassigned to the FBI Headquarters in Washington, DC. We celebrated Christmas in Avon Lake and a few days later, the Allied Van Lines Moving Company truck showed up to load our furniture. The last item to go on the truck was our Christmas tree. Dad wanted to set it up for New Year's Eve and New Year's Day in our new home in Lorton, Virginia, outside of Washington, DC.

After moving into our new home in Lorton, Dad enjoyed relaxing on New Year's Eve and New Year's Day. It was on that New Year's Eve that we met our new neighbors, Mr. and Mrs. Carlson, an elderly couple who lived next door. The Carlsons brought a tray of homemade frozen peanut butter potato candy as a welcoming gift. It was delicious. Mrs. Carlson gave the recipe to Mom, and she made it a few times during the summer and the following New Year's Eve.

New Year's Eve in 1971 was quite memorable. Our parents had gone out food shopping and to have a nice quiet dinner together. John Jr. was sixteen and allowed to keep an eye on us while they were gone.

THANKSGIVING & CHRISTMAS

Mom, Marie, John, Jim, Dad, Paul
(Neal in front) Christmas 1970s

About a three-to-five-minute walk up the street from our home in Lorton was a Drug and Alcohol Rehabilitation Center. This complex of buildings was originally built in the early 1900s as a prison for women suffragists. While there were no walls or fences around the rehabilitation center, there were guards in guard towers overseeing the property.

The previous summer, while visiting Mom's side of the family in Tennessee, John and Jim had stocked up on all kinds of fireworks. They had what we referred to as "buzz bombs." After lighting a "buzz bomb," it would lift off the ground like a helicopter, making a loud buzzing sound. After reaching a certain height, it exploded.

While our parents were out shopping and having dinner, John, Jim, and I walked up the street and hid behind a bush about fifty yards from one of the guard towers. They told me to crawl across the open lawn area to the base of the guard tower and light the "buzz bomb." After lighting the device, it immediately rose into the sky, lighting up the entire area. I stood up and sprinted away as I heard the "buzz bomb" explode.

After making our way back home, there was a lot of laughter while at the same time being worried that a guard would come knocking on our door. We spent the rest of the evening eating Twinkies and watching a movie titled *Mad Monster Party* featuring the voice of Boris Karloff.

New Year's Eve was one of the few times we were allowed to stay up until midnight to watch the ball fall in Times Square in New York City on TV. I usually fell asleep soon after midnight but enjoyed watching the Dick Clark or Guy Lombardo New Year's Eve Special with family. As I grew into my twenties and beyond, I attended a variety of different New Year's Eve celebrations but returned home for New Year's dinner. Eventually, I started my own tradition of cooking a New Year's dinner for my family.

CHAPTER 14

Family Birthdays

During the late 1950s through the 1960s, our family birthdays were celebrated on the actual birth date regardless of what day of the week it was. Because we lived so far away from relatives, we celebrated birthdays with the immediate family. The only exception to this was on my sister Marie's birthday in July, which we celebrated at our grandmother's house in Tennessee while on vacation visiting Mom's side of the family.

When we were young children, the birthday child received a large present while the other non-birthday children received a small gift. Before our birthdays, Mom asked us what kind of birthday cake we wanted that year. Some of us enjoyed the store-bought birthday cakes, while others wanted one of her homemade cakes. Mom was a great cook and baker.

At some point as a child, I realized that store-bought cakes made life much easier for Mom, so I usually opted for the store-bought cakes. I remember how exciting it was when Dad arrived home with a store-bought cake. It was fun to see the cake through the plastic square window on the top of the box.

Mark - 1st Birthday

FAMILY BIRTHDAYS

Another reason I requested a store-bought cake on my birthday was that I knew I could enjoy her homemade cakes year-round.

John Jr. loved Mom's homemade dream whip cakes. These dream whip cakes consisted of six layers of chocolate separated by layers of a special whipped cream frosting. Jim enjoyed Mom's homemade coconut cakes. Every so often, Mom would buy a Pepperidge Farm Coconut Cake at the grocery store just for Jim.

Our family birthday celebrations were simple but memorable. After dinner, Mom would light the candles on the cake in the kitchen while one of us children volunteered to shut the dining room lights off when instructed to do so. For whatever reason, being chosen to turn off the lights prior to presenting the cake became competitive. There were a few occasions when my younger brothers and sister cried if they weren't chosen, so our parents quickly learned to choose the youngest children for the task.

Once the candles were lit, Mom would shout, "Turn the lights off" and walk into the dining room with the lit candles on the cake while prompting us to sing *Happy Birthday*. She would set the cake in front of the birthday child, and after the singing was complete, he or she would blow out the candles and make a wish, then receive the first piece of cake and a scoop of ice cream. After everyone finished their cake and ice cream, usually Neapolitan, gifts were given out. As previously mentioned, even if it wasn't your birthday, you still received a small, inexpensive gift.

I remember one birthday celebration when we were all young and each of us boys, John, Jim, Mark, and Paul, received a cap gun. I believe it was Marie's birthday party. The price tag for one of those cap guns was ten cents. These cap guns used little rolls of paper caps that could be loaded into the gun and fired, making little pops and sparks. We had hours of fun running around the house while hiding and shooting at each other.

As I look back at our early childhood birthday celebrations, I appreciate the simplicity and bonding that took place within our family. Our parents allowed us the opportunity to see and learn how important it was to appreciate and enjoy someone else's special day.

CHAPTER 15

FBI Family Gatherings & Events

It was fun to attend FBI-sponsored family events and cookouts during the 1960s. There was a special relationship and comfort level between the FBI agent families associated with the Cleveland office.

One of Dad's friends and fellow agents, Mr. Weber, lived on the other side of the duplex we lived in at 3371 Thoreau Road in Lakewood, Ohio. Mr. and Mrs. Webber had two daughters, Dawn, who was John's age and Sherry, Jim's age. The wall separating the attics of the duplex was incomplete, so John and Jim could talk to Dawn and Sherry through the thin wall at a certain vantage point. Sherry was in Jim's kindergarten class at Garfield Elementary School. They would talk about safety class, where they learned how to walk along and cross the busy streets in the area.

Joe Nealon was another agent and friend of Dad's. The Nealon family included a son named Mike, a daughter known as "Cookie" (Mary), and an older daughter employed at the Cleveland FBI Headquarters. Dad occasionally gave her rides to and from work if Mr. Nealon had to be elsewhere. Mr. Nealon, along with Mike, sometimes went fishing with us. The Nealons often came to our home in Avon Lake for cookouts during the summer months. Jim recalls Mr. Nealon and Mike coming to our house and helping Dad patch a leaky spot on our roof.

Agent Quill was another friend of Dad's. Jim remembers Dad telling him that if you ever meet anyone with the last name Quill, they are most likely related to Mr. Quill because it was a rare name.

Agent John Farren was a special friend of Dad's. Mr. Farren died at a young age, perhaps in the line of duty. He once told Dad he had planted a tree in the yard near every house he had ever owned. Dad adopted the custom by planting trees in our yards in Avon Lake, Ohio, Lorton, Virginia, and Grafton, Massachusetts.

Jim Berg, or "Bergen," was an agent who lived with his family in a neighboring town. One Saturday afternoon, Dad took us to visit Mr. Bergen and his family. Jim recalls how well-behaved Mr. Bergen's kids were and how astonished they were when we informed them that rotten apples lying on the ground could be used as weapons in a game we called "apple wars." Playing "apple wars" was a childhood tradition where every fall we divided ourselves up into two teams and threw rotten apples at each other.

There were a few occasions when we went to Euclid Beach Amusement Park in Cleveland with other FBI agent families. Euclid Beach Amusement Park opened on June 22, 1895, offering a beach, swimming, fishing, picnic tables, a bathhouse, a dance hall, a theater, and a roller-skating rink. During the early years, the park offered alcoholic drinks, freak shows and gambling. In 1901, Dudley S. Humphries, a religious and family man, converted the park to make it more appealing to families and respectable guests.

The first time I went to Euclid Beach Amusement Park, we waited outside the main gate for other FBI agent families to arrive. The plan was to meet outside the main entry gate and enter as a large group. Once everyone had arrived, the adults purchased and handed out ride tickets to all of us children. We were told to have fun and meet at the picnic area for lunch around noontime. I have no idea what our parents did while we ran around the park and enjoyed the amusements. Back in those days, it was safe to let your kids run free and have fun.

My most memorable attractions at the park were the old creaky wooden roller coaster and the Surprise House. The Surprise House was a fun house considered by many to be dangerous and risky. It had moving bridges and trick floors that made people trip and fall. Prior to entering the Surprise House, a mechanical robot named Laughing Sal greeted you. She swayed back and forth while laughing obnoxiously. Some viewed Sal as funny, and others found her creepy. I never liked Laughing Sal, who still appears in my nightmares every so often.

I regularly experienced a few bumps and bruises while walking through the Surprise House. An attraction such as this would not be allowed in our society today. After exiting the Surprise House, there was a kiosk with a sign prompting you to press a button to make a mechanical mouse go to a piece of cheese. This small attraction never worked the few times I pressed the button.

My worst experience at Euclid Beach Amusement Park was on a ride called The Rotor. This was a circular, barrel-shaped ride where a person entered and stood on a short ledge about one foot long to wait for the ride to start spinning. As the ride progressed faster, the shelf you were standing on withdrew to the point where you would stick to the wall by force of friction combined with inertia. I was so afraid of falling and could not understand why I had not. It was approximately twenty feet to the floor below. I was horrified as the ride slowed down, fearful I would fall. Finally, I slid along the wall to the bottom of the barrel and quickly exited.

As directed by our parents, families would meet at the picnic area around noon to enjoy lunch. Mom packed the most amazing bologna and cheese sandwiches, potato chips, and soda pop. I can remember arriving home later in the afternoon, exhausted and tired from the fun and excitement.

Another popular amusement park where agents and their families met was Cedar Point Amusement Park in Sandusky, Ohio. We loved going to Cedar Point and had a great family outing there whenever we went.

I think Dad's favorite attraction at Cedar Point was the train ride with mechanical skeleton props. Dad constantly had a smile on his face as we watched the mechanical skeletons in action. A few wore firefighter costumes, pretending to fight fires, while others were cowboys acting out a gunfight. In 1964, Cedar Point built a wooden roller coaster called The Blue Streak. It was the highlight of my trip to Cedar Point, and I would ride it seven or eight times while there. The Blue Streak is still in use today.

FBI Family Picnic 1958

We enjoyed the FBI family picnics organized at different parks in the Cleveland area. There were also private cookouts held at many of the agents' private residences. The agents worked together cooking hot dogs and hamburgers while the wives set up tables and put out homemade potato and macaroni salad. Mom made the best potato salad using an old Southern recipe she learned from her mother. There were homemade cookies, cupcakes, and plenty of ice-cold "pop."

Dad once told me that some agents living in Cleveland enjoyed coming to our house in Avon Lake because their kids could play in our huge backyard and apple orchard. We had an excellent fire pit for cooking marshmallows and large fields to run around and play in. In the evening, we watched the thousands of fireflies brighten the area. I typically burned my marshmallows at first, but I soon found out they tasted fantastic.

When Dad learned he was being promoted and transferred to the FBI Headquarters in Washington, DC, he took the whole family to the Tropicana Restaurant for pizza. The Tropicana was located right up the street at the end of Moore Road, next to Lake Erie. This was one of the few times our whole family went out to dinner together at a restaurant. I was excited yet nervous after learning that we were moving to Virginia because I would be entering the second half of sixth grade at a different school.

As I look back, having parents who worked for the FBI created a unique family situation. There was a sense of comfort hanging out with other FBI families. Everyone had a special understanding, which made getting together more relaxing and fun.

CHAPTER 16

Avon Lake, Ohio
(1965-1970)

One reason our parents left the city and moved to Avon Lake, Ohio, was to get away from the racial riots and social unrest that were taking place in Cleveland during the early to mid-1960s. We moved to an old farmhouse that was built in 1844 by one of the early settlers of Avon Lake. After conducting research on the history of the property, I learned that a German immigrant whose last name was Urig bought the land and constructed the farmhouse we lived in a short distance from Lake Erie and next to French Creek.

270 Moore Road – Avon Lake, Ohio

Urig worked on fishing boats and grew wheat in the enormous field behind the house. He built a small barn where he could keep two horses to pull his plow and his buggy for transportation.

He planted eight to ten apple trees, black walnut trees, and established a small grape vineyard on the other side of French Creek. Urig planted blackberry bushes along the edge of the wheat field.

AVON LAKE, OHIO (1965-1970)

There was a small convenience store north of our house called Lawson's. We could easily walk or ride bikes to this store to buy milk, bread, and candy. A short distance westward from Lawson's was a small plaza with a Ben Franklin Five & Ten Store and a small corner drugstore. In the same plaza was an old building that was originally built to serve as the Avon Lake Power Plant and Beach Park Station. This was where people working at the Cleveland Electric Illuminating Company or visiting the Avon Lake Beach Park for recreation could access the electric train.

In 1949, a section of the old electric train station was converted into the Avon Lake Theater. A different section of the train station became the Saddle Inn & Restaurant.

At the north end of Moore Road, there was a fishing bait facility and boat rental business along with the Tropicana Restaurant. I had fun exploring this part of our neighborhood.

Mom enjoyed having a vegetable garden. In the spring of 1966, Dad made a garden behind our small red barn. He planted corn, pumpkins, and green beans. I could tell Dad was working hard "tilling" the soil with a shovel, so I offered to help.

The barn was a fun place to play and decorate for Halloween. We played touch football and kick the can in our large backyard. We built a fort next to the creek, behind our apple orchard, and made a fire pit using large stones.

Living in Avon Lake, Ohio, was exciting, and it was a fun place to be a child in the mid to late 1960s. I will never forget the memories we made there as a family.

CHAPTER 17

The Lorton Years

Lorton, Virginia (December 1970—April 1972)

Our new residence, located at 9402 Ox Road in Lorton, Virginia, was constructed in the 1920s using red bricks produced at a nearby historic brick factory in the quaint village of Occoquan. The original builders constructed the house for workers and their families who were employed in the Lorton Prison System. The house was in beautiful condition and perfect for our family of nine.

9402 Ox Road – Lorton, VA

John and Jim shared a large bedroom, and Paul and I had our own spacious one. Neal and Rich shared their own large bedroom, while Marie had her own small private suite. Mom and Dad had their own bedroom on the first floor with a private bathroom and built-in wall safe. There was an additional bathroom on the first floor, and another on the second floor. The kitchen was large with a walk-in pantry. Mom loved the kitchen and pantry. She liked the fact that our new home was about the same distance from her family in Tennessee and my dad's family in Massachusetts.

The house had a moderate-sized dining room, a long rectangle living room and a small music room with double glass doors. At the front of the house, there was a screened porch, and behind the home was a large garage with a second floor. It was a spot for us to relax and play games.

Sometimes during warm weather, Mom and Dad let us older kids sleep out in the garage on the second floor. This was fun to do in the fall. We lit Halloween candles and told ghost stories. The basement was spacious and had an old 1920s washing machine that was left behind by the previous owners. The side yard was large and a perfect place to play touch football on Thanksgiving.

The woods behind our home were endless and belonged to the Lorton Prison System. There were old dirt roads, which spanned for miles and miles we explored by riding our bikes. It was an excellent location where I could shoot my BB gun and set my handmade box traps. It was in Lorton when Mom first allowed me to take Neal with me when I hiked around the small circular trail in the woods behind the house to shoot my BB gun and check my box traps. I had fun building box traps and releasing the animals after capture.

Mark, Jim, Mom, Paul, Dad, Marie,
Mrs. Carlson, Neal, Mr. Carson
Lorton, Virginia

While in Lorton, John and Jim sometimes did things together or individually. Paul and I enjoyed walking up the street to Hanlin's store to buy candy and soda. We had fun watching late-night, black and white horror movies on Friday and Saturday nights. Occasionally, we hung out with Jeff and Chris, who lived up the street. We enjoyed going to their house to climb around their barn and jump off the top of the hayloft into a pile of hay below.

Jeff and Chris had a minibike. Everyone took turns riding the minibike that was constantly breaking down. Paul and I would ride our bikes to Occoquan to fish in the river or to jump off the Occoquan Bridge and swim during the hot summer months.

While our family was formally registered with Our Lady of Angels Catholic Church in Woodbridge, Virginia, we occasionally attended Mass at St. Mary of Sorrows Catholic Church in Fairfax. This was a small, historic church that attracted many tourists.

In early September 1862, after the second battle of Manassas, Clara Barton helped transport over 3000 soldiers from the battlefield to the church and surrounding homes for medical assistance. That cold winter, the pews in the church were used to build beds and burnt as firewood to keep the wounded warm.

After the war, President Ulysses S. Grant ordered new pews to be installed in the church. I thought it was interesting to be sitting in the pews during Mass while thinking about Clara Barton and the many wounded soldiers she cared for.

While living in Virginia, John went to Springfield High School in Springfield, Virginia, Jim was a student at Washington Irving Intermediate Junior High School and Springfield High School, I completed the second half of sixth grade at Lorton Elementary School and most of seventh grade at Washington Irving Intermediate Junior High School. Paul, Marie, and Neal attended Lorton Elementary School while Rich was not of school age yet.

While in sixth grade at Lorton Elementary School, my teacher planned with Dad to come to the FBI Headquarters for a special field trip and private tour. These kinds of tours were rarely allowed. The only reason our class was permitted to have a private tour of the headquarters was because of Dad's position.

Upon our arrival, our school bus pulled up to the large steel entry gates that led into the underground parking garage. After the gates opened, our bus driver entered the secured garage and was instructed to remain on the bus until an agent arrived to provide further directions. Five minutes later, an elevator door opened. Dad, along with three other men, exited and walked toward us as they waved and smiled. They stood outside the bus talking for a minute or two until the three men waved again and walked back to the elevator. I later learned that one of the men was J. Edgar Hoover.

Next, Dad allowed the bus driver and our teacher to exit the bus and talked for about five minutes. We were then told we could all get off the bus, and Dad introduced himself to the students in my class. We started our tour by visiting the evidence room, which was in the building's basement, close to where we were. I had been to the evidence room with Dad prior to this field trip and thought it was even more interesting the second time.

After leaving the evidence room, we took the elevator up to the first floor and were given a presentation in the fingerprint room. This was amazing. Dad pointed out a new fingerprint laser technology machine that could pull fingerprints off objects thirty to forty years after the prints had been made.

We departed the fingerprint room and were heading to the FBI firearms vault when alarms started going off throughout the building. Agents were scrambling and running up and down the hallways while Dad calmly told us we needed to return to the bus. We were told to board the bus and wait for further instructions. Ten minutes later, Dad and nine other armed agents, all carrying machine guns, surrounded the bus. Dad calmly told my teacher and bus driver that there were hundreds of anti-war protesters surrounding the building and they were going to escort us out of the garage to the main road. He told the bus driver to go as slowly as possible.

As the gates opened, we exited the building with ten armed agents walking alongside the bus. The protesters looked surprised and ran away. As soon as we made it to the top of the entrance driveway, Dad waved, and the agents calmly walked backward into the parking garage. I saw my teacher looking stunned and gazing forward as the gate shut.

I thought what had happened was so cool, and the kids in my class later told me they wanted to be FBI agents someday. Dad came to my school the following week and spoke to my class about careers in the FBI. I became popular at school after the incident.

While stationed in Washington, Dad was busy reviewing potential FBI investigations for the East Coast region of the United States. Occasionally, he left the office to handle investigations taking place in DC or to deliver confidential messages from Hoover to Nixon at the White House.

Dad once told me about a situation involving a Russian spy working in the DC area. Hoover wanted the Russian spy apprehended, so he assigned Dad and another top agent to conduct surveillance and make an arrest when the spy exchanged American military secrets with his contact. Dad and the other agent were able to locate and take photos of the suspect and followed him to a restaurant in downtown Washington. To their surprise, the spy sat down and started having lunch with Hoover.

The Lorton Drug and Rehab Center Guard Tower

This was an interesting situation, and Dad did not want Hoover to see them conducting surveillance through the large window overlooking the outside of the restaurant. Dad's theory was that the spy had somehow tricked Hoover into meeting him for lunch, pretending to be an American official. In the surveillance report, Dad and the other agent wrote that they saw the spy having lunch at the restaurant with an "unidentified" person. Dad told me this story on multiple occasions and thought it was hilarious. As far as Dad knew, Hoover never found out he was under surveillance. Most likely, Hoover did not know he was having lunch with a Russian spy.

Mom and Dad would go food shopping at the Super Giant Supermarket at Marumsco Plaza in Woodbridge, Virginia, every Friday night. To get to the town of Woodbridge, you had to drive over an old one-lane steel bridge that crossed the Occoquan River. People had to take turns crossing the bridge, but it was never an issue.

Mom would take "baby" Richard along with them on their shopping trip, while the rest of us were allowed to stay home with John, who was around sixteen years old. We were allowed to hang out in and around the house and told not to leave the yard. Mom and Dad would come home with eight or ten bags of groceries and enough food for dinners for the next seven days. Dad bought a large freezer, which was placed on the back porch to store frozen food for the week. When they arrived home with the groceries, we all ran outside and helped unload the car. We also helped put the groceries in the pantry so we could see the special treats that were purchased. We looked forward to Nutty Buddy Ice Cream Cones, Dolly Madison Chocolate Cupcakes, Hostess Twinkies, Little Debbie Swiss Rolls, Popsicles, and Pepperidge Farm Cakes, to name a few.

Living in Lorton was exciting and adventurous. I later learned that one reason we left Lorton was because of the prison riots that were occurring up the street at the Lorton Maximum Security Prison. The second reason was that our home was only a few hundred yards from the Lorton Drug & Alcohol Rehabilitation Center, where patients were free to roam the area. The third reason was that Dad wanted to work in Boston and live in the Worcester area to be near his family. Dad and Mom did a great job locating a beautiful home at 5 Virginia Circle in Grafton, Massachusetts, that offered a safe community and friendly neighborhood.

CHAPTER 18

Grafton (1970s)

Moving from Lorton, Virginia, to Grafton, Massachusetts, was exciting and allowed Dad the opportunity to be near his sisters, Irene and Edna. Dad did his research and wanted to find a home in a small town away from the problems associated with cities. I remember arriving about a week before the April 1, 1972 closing date on our new home at 5 Virginia Circle.

We stayed at the Holiday Inn on Main Street in Worcester, anxiously waiting to move into our house. I remember the Neal Young song, *Heart of Gold*, was constantly played on the radio and Willy Wonka candy was popular. There were many department stores on Main Street, and Mom enjoyed exploring the area while pushing Richard in a stroller.

I'll never forget walking into our home at 5 Virginia Circle for the first time after closing. While the house was not as large as our home in Virginia, it worked out well for our family of nine. John and Jim had their own bedroom with a window that allowed access to

5 Virginia Circle – Grafton, Massachusetts

the flat roof on the side porch and the staircase to the attic. John and Jim made a small reading room in the attic.

Paul and I had our own bedroom at the top of the stairs with windows overlooking the creek and backyard. Neal and Richard shared a bedroom with a fancy English-style window facing the street at the front of the house. Marie had her own small bedroom with a window overlooking the side yard and street. Marie had to access her bedroom by first going through Neal and Richard's bedroom door. Mom and Dad had their own bedroom on the first floor. There were two bathrooms, one on the first floor and another on the second floor. The kitchen and dining room were small, while the living room was large.

There was another room on the first floor that we used as a place to watch television. This room had a door leading out to a shaded screened porch. The porch became a popular place to make puzzles, read books, carve pumpkins or take a quiet nap. The basement became a music room and a place to enjoy board games or watch television. This was where our band, *Slant 6 and the Jumpstarts,* originated. We never used the garage for automobiles, but it became a work area with tools and lawn equipment. There were woods behind the house where we hunted and made campfires. This was a great place where Neal and Rich could play.

Basement at Virginia Circle

Dad enjoyed his commute from Grafton to the FBI Headquarters in Boston. It was easy to access the Massachusetts Turnpike by traveling through North Grafton to Millbury. He would leave around 5:00 a.m. and meet some of the other agents at the Boston YMCA to run a mile and play basketball. After working out, he took a shower and went out for breakfast with the other agents before reporting to the office. He normally returned home anywhere between 5:30 p.m. and 7:00 p.m. and had dinner with the family.

Grafton was a fantastic town, and Virginia Circle offered an excellent neighborhood for kids. Mom and Dad became good friends with Bud and Lynn Holland, who lived two houses up the street. Dad played on the Klondike Inn Softball Team with Bud Holland on Sundays. Dad was an excellent pitcher and enjoyed playing in the league. Mr. and Mrs. Holland had four children: Ken, Laura, Tom, and Paul.

A few days after moving into our new home, I saw Ken Holland standing in front of the sewer grate at the corner of our street, kicking pebbles into it. I walked over and started talking with him and began kicking pebbles into the sewer grate as well. With that interaction, we began getting to know each other. We are still friends to this day. Marie became friends with Laura Holland, while Neal and Rich played with Tom and Paul Holland. Every so often, Mr. and Mrs. Holland had a small cocktail party with some of their friends and invited Mom and Dad.

Interestingly, Dad and Bud enjoyed the challenges associated with fixing cars. Whenever there was a car on Virginia Circle with an open hood or up on a jack, Dad or Bud would show up and assist with the repairs. I remember people in our neighborhood saying, "John and Bud could fix anything with a roll of duct tape and an empty soup can." We couldn't have landed in a better neighborhood.

Mr. and Mrs. Mancuso were a young couple who lived directly across the street. Mr. Mancuso is the co-owner of Mancuso & Nowak Insurance Agency on Route 9 in Shrewsbury, Massachusetts. He was a great neighbor and constantly ready to help our family with things like car insurance and registration. Occasionally, I saw Mr. Mancuso when he worked out at the Catalina Health Club in Shrewsbury, Massachusetts. We were excited to see Mr. and Mrs. Mancuso when they drove their

1947 Woody in and out of Virginia Circle when going for a Sunday drive. They were fantastic neighbors.

At about the same time I met and became friends with Ken Holland, I met Doug Walsh, who lived in the house on Worcester Street right behind and next to the Hollands' home on Virginia Circle. I remember Doug coming over with a baseball and mitt and asking me if I wanted to play catch. We played catch for about an hour while talking about things to do in Grafton. Doug's younger brother was Neal's age, and they too became friends.

Mr. and Mrs. Chartier lived on Worcester Street, a few houses up from the entrance of Virginia Circle. They had four children, Jack, Jim, Danny, and Sue. My brother Jim became friends with Jack Chartier. I became friends with Jim Chartier, while Marie became friends with Sue Chartier. Danny Chartier did not align age-wise with any of the Ouellettes but was still considered a good friend of our family.

Vinnie Caracciolo

At age fourteen, I attended Firearms Safety School with my new friends, Ken Holland, Jim Chartier, and Doug Walsh. Vinnie Caracciolo, the game warden who lived in Grafton and worked out of his office in Westborough, Massachusetts, was the instructor for the class. Once a student passed the class, they received a temporary firearms identification card that allowed you to carry a shotgun or 22 caliber rifles when hunting or target shooting as long as you were accompanied by an adult eighteen years of age or older who carried a firearms identification card. I did not realize it, but Dad had already met and become friends with Mr. Caracciolo. I am not sure what the policy is today, but back in the 1970s, Massachusetts State Police, local police, and game wardens were required to purchase their own personal ammunition for target practice. Federal agents were not required to pay for personal ammunition. Every so often, Dad stopped by and dropped off ammunition at the Grafton State Police barracks, the Grafton Police Station and the Game Warden Headquarters in Westborough, Massachusetts. This was how he met Vinnie Caracciolo.

After turning fifteen, I could hunt and target practice on my own. This was when Dad started bringing me cases of 12- and 20-gauge shotgun shells. I had a great time hunting and target shooting in the woods behind our house.

There was an incident that occurred in the early 1970s, not too long after we moved to Grafton, when Dad and another agent had arrested a person who was running an illegal gambling ring and confiscated approximately $144,000.00. Following the arrest, Dad and his partner were sitting at a table counting the money while a photographer secretly took their picture. The photo of Dad and the other agent counting the money appeared on the front page of a Springfield newspaper. Hoover did not approve of photographers taking pictures of federal agents for security and safety reasons. In addition, the photographer broke traditional law enforcement/journalist etiquette.

I remember Dad coming home and telling Mom that we might be packing up and leaving soon. There was concern that this picture in the newspaper could cause some kind of retaliation against Dad and possibly members of our family. Fortunately, we did not need to move, and there were no issues related to the event.

On July 31, 1973, Delta Flight 723 hit a concrete seawall as it attempted to land at Logan Airport in Boston in the fog. The plane burst into flames, killing almost everyone on board instantly. Fifty-seven passengers boarded the DC-9 plane in Burlington, Vermont, which then flew to the Manchester airport to pick up thirty-two more passengers after their flight was canceled due to fog. Fortunately, for one man who had already boarded the plane in Manchester, he realized he was going to miss his meeting in New York and begged the pilot to let him off the plane. This was his lucky day.

When Dad and the other agents from the Boston office arrived at the scene, they discovered the plane had almost completely disintegrated from the fire. Dad and the other agents at the crash scene collected burnt and charred body parts and any remaining wreckage for the investigation. It was determined that the belly of the plane struck the seawall as it attempted to land in the fog, and it was ruled an accident.

There were six severely burned survivors when rescuers arrived, but five of them died on the way to the hospital, while the other person died on December 11, over three months after the accident. Dad went to visit this survivor a few times during that three-month period.

As previously mentioned, Dad enjoyed driving to and from Boston. It was a time to relax and listen to the radio. The 1969 Chevy Townsman Wagon he drove had air conditioning and comfortable seats. After John Jr. received his driver's license, Dad bought a second vehicle. He wanted a car that was gas efficient and FBI approved. He purchased a green Plymouth Valiant with a slant-six engine. Eventually, this car earned the nickname "The Green Box."

Having a second automobile allowed John the opportunity to drive the station wagon back and forth to college and work. In addition, he could drive Mom to the grocery store and other destinations. Jim used the station wagon occasionally after obtaining his driver's license. Eventually, Jim bought his own first car, a 1968 Dodge Polaris. I was able to drive the wagon a few times after obtaining my driver's license until John "totaled it" in an accident in front of the Massachusetts Turnpike entrance in Millbury. Fortunately, John escaped unharmed and decided to purchase his own vehicle.

The best place to apply for a car loan back in the seventies was the Grafton Credit Union. Charlie Bolack, founder and president of the credit union, was popular and ever willing to help fellow Grafton residents. I needed to buy a car on two occasions, and I remember walking into the credit union and hearing Charlie shout from behind the counter, "How's your dad?" followed by, "How much do you need?"

Dad was invited to take part in a few "Career Day" events held at Grafton High School in the early and mid-1970s. Students were fascinated by the fact that an FBI agent was at the event. One of my teachers told me that there had never been an FBI agent participating in the Career Day. Our principal, Mr. LeMay, was involved in reaching out and inviting Dad to the Career Day event. Mr. LeMay was a great principal and role model.

While living in Grafton during the 1970s, I enjoyed going fishing at Lake Ripple. I never kept the fish because of known water pollution problems. I also liked to go hunting in the woods behind our house and in other wooded areas around Grafton. One morning before school, I shot seven pheasants up in the fields near Fay Mountain Road. It took me a few hours to gut and pluck the pheasants, so I had to go to school late that day.

As I had done in Virginia, I continued digging up and collecting old bottles I found behind old stone walls. I once discovered old coins in small metal canisters hidden in a stone wall in the woods behind our house. Someone must have hidden the coins there many years ago, and either forgot where they were or died. There were about a hundred coins in the container, dating back to the 1800s.

During the early and mid-1970s, I played basketball at Norcross Park in Grafton Center as much as possible. This was where I met John Harrington, who invited me to work out with weights in his parents' basement three or four days a week after playing basketball. Mr. and Mrs. Harrington let me come over and work out, even if their son, John, was not at home. Mr. Harrington often had me over to hang out at his pool, to listen to the Red Sox and relax. He never hesitated to put me to work in the garden.

As I reflect on my life living in Grafton during the 1970s, I remember sharing telephone party lines with other households in the area. If someone was using the line you shared and there was an emergency, you had to ask the people who were talking to hang up so you could make your emergency phone call. Sometimes we picked up the phone, covered the talking end, and listened to other people's conversations. If you laughed too loud, they would ask, "Is someone listening to our conversation?"

Aerial view of Grafton Center 1985

The Massachusetts "Blue Laws" were still in place during the 1970s. The "Blue Laws" mandated that businesses be closed and the sale of alcohol illegal on Sundays. I liked the fact that businesses were closed on Sundays, making life slow down a little bit once a week. We often went to Paul's Produce to buy beer on Sundays.

GRAFTON (1970S)

Some of the popular destinations we frequented while living in Grafton during the 1970s included The Mart, Kings Supermarket, Tasty Pizza, Grafton Pizza, The Wonder Bar, The Woodshed Restaurant, and the Grafton Flea Market. Some of the popular destinations outside of Grafton were The Tanela Polynesian Chinese Restaurant on Route 20, the Edgemere Drive-In Theater, and the Westboro Speedway. Grafton was a town where most people knew or had heard of each other. I loved being a teenager in Grafton during the 1970s. In my opinion, life was much simpler and less complicated then.

CHAPTER 19

The Raytheon Years

Between 1970 and 1981, the inflation rate in the United States increased to record highs. We had lived comfortably during the 1950s and 1960s and were able to purchase a home in Grafton at an amazing price in 1972. Less than a year after Dad's retirement from the FBI in 1977, he decided to go back to work to make additional money to meet the challenges of inflation. Our mother also went back to work part time to help with the bills.

Dad made a few phone calls and received a job offer from the Secret Service. He thought about it and declined the job offer because traveling with the Secret Service would keep him away from home while Marie, Neal, and Richard were still in school.

As a graduate of Holy Cross College in Worcester, he considered teaching political science at the college. He was offered the job but received a much higher-paying position with Raytheon Corporation, producers of the Hawk and Patriot missiles in Lexington, Massachusetts. Dad accepted the position of manager of security at the Lexington office.

Soon after accepting this position, he signed a two-year contract to manage security for Americans working for Raytheon in Saudi Arabia. The initial plan was that Dad, along with Mom, Paul, Neal, and Richard, would travel to Saudi Arabia and live in the American Complex. Marie would attend Marymount International School in Rome, Italy. The American compound known as "Rayville" was in the town of Riyadh.

While inside the American Compound, employees could continue living the American lifestyle. However, when an American left the compound, they were under the laws of Saudi Arabia.

Neal and Richard went to the American Elementary School inside the compound while Marie attended Merry Mount in Rome, Italy. Paul, who had recently graduated from Grafton High School and had not yet turned eighteen years of age, worked as a lifeguard at the pool located inside the American compound.

Back at home in Grafton, John and Jim were working full and part-time jobs while taking college classes. I worked part time while transitioning from U-Mass in Amherst to Worcester State College.

We had a neighbor, Jim Dalton, who was renting a room at the house next door. He was invited by our parents to move into our home for free if he kept an "eye" on the property and provided a "check and balance" for our college-partying ways. We nick-named him "Pinto" in honor of the Ford Pinto he drove and his ability to fix cars.

Pinto was a great person and friend who enjoyed drinking beer. He was in his late fifties or early sixties, and we got along well. Pinto liked to go to country and western bars every Friday and Saturday night and didn't return home until one or two in the morning. Tumbleweeds in North Grafton was a popular destination. This allowed us to have some fun parties at the house. Even when Pinto came home early, he would hang out with us.

While in Saudi Arabia, Dad was responsible for the safety and security of the American citizens who worked for Raytheon and lived in the American compound. In addition, he was responsible for the security surrounding the transport of the Hawk and Patriot missiles to installation locations.

There was an incident Dad was involved with surrounding the transport of missiles to a top-secret location about eighty miles north of the American Compound. Dad drove the last car at the back of the procession right behind a truck carrying some missiles. After traveling a short distance across the Arab Desert, the missiles fell off the carrier truck a few hundred yards ahead and began rolling directly toward him. He quickly did a U-turn and pressed down on the pedal, traveling over 140 miles per hour while looking up at his rearview mirror waiting for an explosion. The engine of the car he was driving was so hot it was smoking.

Eventually, when he felt it was safe, and the missiles had stopped rolling, he pulled over by the side of the road and waited a few minutes, observing cautiously from a distance. When he felt it was safe, he returned to assess the damage. Fortunately, no one was hurt, and there were no explosions. The US military soon arrived to secure the area and clean up the mess. It was later determined that the Saudi soldiers at the airport forgot to lock the chains that were holding the missiles on the transport carrier. Dad laughed when telling this story and commented that it was one of the few times he had ever exceeded the speed limit.

Under Sharia (Islamic law), the sale and consumption of alcohol are strictly prohibited in Saudi Arabia. Those caught breaking this law are fined and put in jail. There was an incident when a Raytheon employee living in the American compound attempted to have bottles of whiskey smuggled into the country by having the bottles packed and hidden inside PVC pipes. The man had to go to the airport to retrieve the whiskey from the pipes and bring the "stash" back to the compound. Somehow, the local Saudi police caught him in the act and brought him to the local Saudi police station to await transfer to the Saudi government prison.

Dad quickly reached out to his interpreter, Hussein, and they sped off to the local police station with $140,000.00 to bribe the police guard to allow them to take the employee directly to the airport and get him out of the country. Fortunately, this worked out for the employee, and soon after, Dad brought the man's wife and kids to the airport and sent them back to the United States. Upon the man's arrival in the United States, Raytheon representatives greeted him and fired him on the spot. They let the man know how lucky he was to have been rescued from the local Saudi jail, avoiding twenty to thirty years in the government prison. They also made him aware that he had cost the company $140,000.00 but would not be required to pay it back.

Women, while inside the American compound in Saudi Arabia, were not required to cover their faces in public. If a female left the compound, she was required by Saudi law to cover her face. Mom did not like this law but followed it to avoid being beaten and arrested. There was also the possibility of being "corralled" by Saudi soldiers without prior notice to observe public punishments. This included men, women, and children of any age in the area.

On one occasion, Mom was out in public with Neal and Richard, who were still in elementary school. Saudi soldiers directed them to observe one of these punishments. The soldiers guided them to stand with the other people in the immediate area in a circular formation around a wooden chopping block where a convicted thief was going to have his hand cut off using an ax. Mom took a chance and distracted Neal and Rich by covering their eyes for the few seconds as the axe struck the man's wrist. Her plan worked because everyone, including the Saudi soldiers, were focused on the chopping block as the ax struck.

Soon after this stressful event, Mom and Dad decided that this was not the best place for Neal and Richard to live. As a result, Mom, Paul, Neal and Rich returned home to Grafton while Dad fulfilled his overseas two-year contract. Dad did come home for Christmas and New Year's, as well as other special occasions. Interestingly, there were a few occasions when Dad flew on the Concorde jet when coming home to visit. Marie returned from Merry Mount School that December at the end of the semester.

After Dad completed his two-year Saudi Arabia contract, he continued working for Raytheon and was promoted to Head of Security for all Raytheon offices and plants in Massachusetts. After ten years working for Raytheon, he was able to draw a second pension along with his federal pension.

One time, Dad invited his interpreter, Hussain, to visit us at our home in the United States. Hussain was a fantastic interpreter, but when he came to visit us in Grafton, he experienced cultural shock. Hussain was in his early to mid-twenties and spoke excellent English. He was a member of a wealthy Saudi oil family.

When Hussain arrived at our home in Grafton, he had a few hundred thousand dollars in one of his suitcases. Dad told him he should not walk around the streets with that much cash. The next morning, Dad brought him to the Grafton Credit Union and helped him open an account. I have no doubt that Charlie Bolack, owner and founder of the Grafton Credit Union, was surprised. Dad allowed Hussain to keep $5,000.00 in his possession for any expenses.

Since Hussain was in his early to mid-twenties, he got along well with John, Jim, Paul, Marie, and me. Dad felt comfortable letting Hussain go out and about the Worcester area with us and, in my opinion, was thankful that we could help keep him "occupied." Hussain told us that blue jeans were scarce in Saudi Arabia, so Marie and I took him to "Maurice the Pants Man" in Worcester. Hussain wanted to buy 200 pairs of jeans to bring back to Saudi Arabia. We convinced him to buy just seven or eight pairs because of potential issues he might have going through customs at the airport with 200 pairs of jeans.

Jim and I took him to a bar in Worcester, where he had his first Mai Tai. This was not the best place we could have taken him, and he became so drunk he started shouting, "I want to buy the bar!" We told him that the bar was not for sale. We took him back to the house later that day and had him go upstairs and take a nap. He woke up at around 5:00 p.m. the *next* afternoon feeling sick from the alcohol and wanted to go out again that evening. Dad was happy to take Hussain to the airport and get him back to Saudi Arabia after the week-long visit.

Dad had an Arab assistant named Mahmud, who came to visit a short time after Hussain returned to Saudi Arbia. Mahmud was older than Hussain and more relaxed. He and Dad enjoyed hanging out and talking. We did not offer to take him to local bars, having learned our lesson with Hussain.

Dad did not like being away from the family, but wanted to honor his two-year contract with Raytheon. He asked me to encourage and support Neal and Richard with their sports and hobbies while he was gone. Despite the challenges of being a full-time college student and working part time, I did the best I could. Fortunately, Neal and Rich had plenty of friends to hang out with at school and in the neighborhood.

Overall, Dad enjoyed the ten years he worked for Raytheon. He made some nice friends that he continued to stay in contact with over the years following his retirement in 1988.

CHAPTER 20

John Norman Jr. Ouellette

Our mother gave birth to John Jr. at Mary Immaculate Hospital in New York City on May 9, 1955. He was baptized at Saint Robert Bellarmine Church on May 22, thirteen days later.

John Jr.

John had many hobbies and interests as a young child and teenager. He enjoyed science, technology, the space program, photography, playing guitar, and following the cultural revolution that was taking place in America. John enjoyed listening to the radio, participating in science fairs, scanning different frequencies on his ham radio, playing records, recording on his quarter inch reel-to-reel tape machine and socializing with friends. He was a dedicated participant in the Cub and Boy Scouts.

John Jr. attended kindergarten at Garfield Elementary and St. Rose Elementary School in Lakewood, Ohio. During the early and mid-1960s, John created and organized unique games. One of these games was called "army." We would divide into two teams, the Americans and the Germans, and then run around with our toy guns, pretending to be engaged in battle.

John Sr. & John Jr. at Hoover Dam 1957

Another game John created was called "dirt clod wars." When the ground was dry in the backyard of our home in Avon Lake, we would gather at the edge of the field. John would stand with his back to the field, holding a spade shovel while closing his eyes and counting to twenty. This was to give us enough time to run into the field and lay down and attempt to hide. After the count to twenty, John would turn around and dig up a clod of dirt and launch it into the field where he believed we might be hiding. When it struck the ground, it created a small dust-like cloud that looked like an atomic bomb mushroom cloud.

The object of the game was to avoid being hit by the dirt clod. Little did we know, John could see the tall grass moving where we were hiding. When John successfully hit a "target," everyone else knew because the person who was hit would moan and groan in agony. I remember being hit only once or twice.

John was an excellent guitar player. He enjoyed listening to the radio and learning how to play his favorite songs. Some bands he liked to listen to include The Beatles, Jimi Hendrix, Crosby, Stills, Nash and Young, King Crimson, Vanilla Fudge and the Monkeys, to name a few.

John and my brother Jim enjoyed listening to their ham radio, which they kept in their bedroom. It was interesting listening to people communicate in foreign languages and not understanding

**Lois, John Sr., & John Jr.
Capitol Building DC 1956**

what was being said. A few times, they invited me to join the listening session. I learned from John and Jim that a person needed a Ham Radio License to transmit or speak to someone using a ham radio. A license is not required to listen. John was eventually granted a Citizens Radio Station License on June 30, 1970.

John enjoyed communicating with other people on his CB radio (Citizens Band Radio), a short-range radio voice communications system commonly used by truckers and individuals in automobiles. I remember how excited John and Jim were when Dad took them to a store that sold crystals for CB radios. Crystals in CB radios can be exchanged, allowing access to different frequencies.

John Jr. & Jim 115th Street Cleveland, Ohio 1959

SCHOOL DAYS 1961-62
ST. ROSE

**John Jr. Grade 2
Lakewood, OH**

John liked to read *Popular Mechanics, Highlights Magazine, and National Geographic.* He spent some of his time assembling and operating his train set and expanded its rail line and landscape. He enjoyed conducting experiments with his science and chemistry kits, stargazing with his telescope, and making model rockets. His favorite models to build were ones that related to the Mercury, Gemini, and Apollo Space Programs. John was known to take apart and put back together electronic devices just to better understand how the devices functioned.

John was creative when recording and producing skits and radio shows on his quarter-inch, reel-to-reel tape machine. Occasionally, he recorded himself talking and playing his favorite music, as if he were "live" on the radio. He transferred some recordings to a cassette and mailed them to our friends. John would also record himself playing songs on his guitar. When in the mood, he was quite creative using Dad's 8 mm and Super 8 film cameras to make short three-minute movies.

John was talking about the Beatles' upcoming performance on the Ed Sullivan Show weeks before the live event on February 9, 1964. Mom and Dad liked to watch The Ed Sullivan Show, and it became a Sunday family ritual. I was almost six, but remember that evening well.

Every Sunday before the start of the Ed Sullivan Show, Dad walked down to the corner drugstore to buy cigarettes. Before leaving, he would ask us what we wanted as a treat from the candy section. John usually requested a Hershey chocolate bar. Jim liked Bun Candy Clusters, while I preferred a Pay Day candy bar. Paul requested a Snickers or Milky Way bar.

On the evening of the first Beatles performance on the Ed Sullivan Show, the whole family sat down on the couch or on the floor and waited patiently for the show to begin. When the Beatles were introduced, I could not believe the way the girls in the audience reacted. They were screaming, crying and fainting as the Beatles performed. As I looked around the room, I noticed John and Jim lightly tapping their feet to the music. Mom and Dad sat quietly and watched. I spent more time watching everyone else's reaction than the show itself. When the performance was over, Dad said, "I think they need haircuts."

During the 1960s, Dad gave us haircuts every few weeks. We nicknamed these haircuts "buzz heads." I did not mind having a "buzz head," but John became resistant over time, searching for ways to allow our parents to let him grow his hair longer. Eventually, our mother took over the haircutting duties and slowly allowed our hair to grow a little longer. By the late 1960s, John was trying to grow sideburns, but Dad would tell him to shave.

The 1960s in America was a time of extreme cultural change. Clothing was becoming more colorful and expressive. Hair was getting longer and shaving less common among the youth. Rock music was becoming experimental and psychedelic. Many artists and musicians focused on the anti-war and civil rights movements. Under the direction of Hoover, FBI agents were trained to better understand the problems and changes that were taking place with the youth in America. I remember seeing some interesting documents on Dad's desk that defined hippie slang. This was to help agents to better communicate with this "new generation."

In the mid-1960s, Dad helped John create a secret room in the basement that was used as a photographic darkroom and a place to keep science and chemistry sets. One day, while exploring the basement, I discovered the secret room. John was so angry I received a "pounding." A pounding was when John put you on the floor face down and pounded your back like a drum with closed fists. It never really hurt but was still something that we younger siblings tried to avoid. I should have stayed out of his secret room and deserved the pounding.

John was a dedicated member of the Cub and Boy Scouts. I remember when both John and Jim went on a weekend camping trip. John was well respected by other members of the troop, and I enjoyed hearing about the pranks they played on each other on these trips.

On at least one occasion, Dad hosted a special trip with some members of the Boy Scout Troop and visited the FBI Headquarters in Cleveland. I was not present, but heard it was fun. We have pictures of John and Jim holding various weapons in the Cleveland FBI Gun Vault.

In the late 1960s, we were allowed to walk up to the Avon Lake Theater on our own to see a movie. John and Jim sat with their friends while Paul and I sat together. There was one Saturday afternoon when parents were allowed to drop their children off at the theater and leave to do errands during the movie.

Imagine a movie theater full of unchaperoned kids. The projectionist would shut off the movie and turn on the lights every so often so the manager could scold us. He informed us that if we did not stop shooting spitballs at each other and at the screen, we would all be kicked out of the theater. I do not think this "drop and shop" matinee program lasted long.

Every fall, St. Joseph's Church held a carnival on an open lawn area next to the church. It was exciting to be allowed to ride the Ferris wheel for the first time with John and Jim. It was at one of these carnivals when I realized how popular John was with girls his age. Girls would run up to him and say hi and then run away. This went on all evening as we walked around the carnival.

L – R Bill, Dean, and John Jr.
at Fort and Fire Pit
in Apple Orchard

Every so often, Dad took us to an Avon Lake High School football game. It was at one of these games when three bullies approached me while standing in line at the concession stand and started pushing me around. After about thirty seconds, one bully said, "That's John Ouellette's little brother!" Suddenly, they stopped pushing me around and quietly walked away. John was bigger and stronger than most kids his age.

John had many friends while living in Avon Lake. One of his best friends was Dean, also known as "Heada." Dean had a large forehead, which inspired the nickname. I remember asking Dean if he liked being called "Heada." He replied, "Yes!"

In nice weather, our parents allowed us to go outside to the fort we built next to French Creek and light a bonfire in the fire pit. It was especially fun in the summer when we would watch thousands of fireflies light up the night. It was relaxing sitting around the fire cooking marshmallows and drinking pop. There were a few times in the late 1960s when I noticed John and Dean passing a small bottle of brandy back and forth. It was fun listening to them talk about different girls they liked at school.

John was a dedicated participant in the Boy Scouts' Pinewood Derby. Scouts would craft miniature race cars out of small blocks of pine and attach wheels. These pinewood cars came in standard kits. The race cars were placed at the top of a downhill slide and released at the same time. The first race car to reach the bottom finish line won.

John proudly marched as a Boy Scout in many of the Avon Lake town parades. These parades were fun to watch as we intently looked for John marching with the rest of the Boy Scout Troop.

When the apples in our small orchard were ripe, we would pick and eat the apples whenever we wanted. Mom used them to make applesauce and apple tarts.

On the darker side, we played a game we called "apple wars." John divided us into two teams. One team occupied the fort we had built next to the creek and was given time to collect apples to store in the "fort" to use as ammunition. The other team assembled and collected apples outside the fort and prepared to attack. The object of the game was to capture or defend the fort, depending on which team you were on. A direct hit from one of those apples could be painful.

John, along with a few other musically talented teenagers, organized a group and performed the first folk Mass at our church. A folk Mass is when traditional liturgical music is substituted with folk music. It was exciting seeing John and other members of the folk group perform during Mass. This helped make Mass more interesting and fun for teenagers.

John was not thrilled when Dad announced we were moving from Avon Lake to Lorton, Virginia, in late December 1970. He was already in high school and had made some close friends in Avon Lake.

JOHN NORMAN JR. OUELLETTE

John Ouellette Jr.

While living in Lorton, John attended West Springfield High School in Springfield, Virginia. He continued to follow the space program and joined the Chemistry Club. While living in Lorton, John inspired me to lift weights. I was in the basement trying to lift his 110-pound plastic weight set when he heard me and came down to see what I was doing. He taught me how to do curls and overhead presses properly. John was twice my size and naturally strong. He could press 200 pounds two or three times. This was my first experience lifting weights.

Moving from Lorton to Grafton, Massachusetts, in April 1972, put our brother John in a unique situation. He was a senior at Springfield High School in Virginia and transferred to Grafton High School a few weeks before graduation. I remember how quickly he adjusted to life in Grafton and how easily he made new friends.

John Jr.
Grafton High School

Soon after moving to Grafton, John started a rock band and performed outside at a few parties in Grafton. He joined the Grafton Fire Department as a Volunteer Fire Fighter and became good friends with another fire department volunteer, Dave Aldrich. Dave became good friends with the Ouellette family. Mom and Dad liked Dave and were happy to see him whenever he came over to our house.

John was active and involved with the Grafton Fire Department. He participated in fire department musters, fundraisers, and chicken barbecues. The memory of our refrigerator overflowing with leftover chicken dinners after the annual chicken barbecue will stay with me forever. Everyone in our family appreciated and enjoyed these leftovers.

John worked part time as a meat cutter at Sentry Supermarket in Millbury, Massachusetts, in the early 1970s. During breaks, they went out onto the parking lot and played street hockey. On certain occasions, Jim made his way to the Sentry Supermarket parking lot to join in the fun.

John worked for a few months at IMCO in South Grafton, Massachusetts, as an injection mold plastics machine operator. He did not stay there long due to the monotony of the job.

John Ouellette Jr. with students
Perkins School for the Blind 1977

John worked at the Perkins School for the Blind in Watertown, Massachusetts, from December 1974 to August 1977. He was a supervisor overseeing deaf-blind and multiple handicapped children in the classroom and living environments. John brought three of his students to our house for Thanksgiving in 1977. I remember John having these kids stand next to each other in the front yard, handing the football back and forth. These kids had such a great time and really enjoyed the experience.

John worked for Suburban Ambulance Company out of Milford, Massachusetts, from August 1977 to August 1978. He took part in several major search and rescue operations including the evacuation of Rockwood, Tennessee, in July 1977, due to a major bromine tank truck spill and a weeklong search for a missing four-year-old boy in Webster, Massachusetts, in October 1978.

In 1979, John worked part time for Delta Air Lines at Logan Airport conducting ramp services. This job included hand signal communication with pilots while parking aircraft, as well as fueling Boeing 727s and L-1011s.

John was interested in the public radio industry. He volunteered as an announcer/engineer at WICN-FM in Worcester, Massachusetts. We had fun listening to him on the radio and making call-in requests.

John became an emergency medical technician, so he was present on the sidelines at my home football games. I remember watching him treat an injured player and thought to myself; *He is really smart!* It was at one of my home football games when I broke one of my fingers, and John, along with another EMT, placed a wooden splint on the injured finger.

They told me they could not use a metal brace because it might cause injury to other players. Dad took me to see Dr. Waters at St. Vincent Hospital that evening and had X-rays of my finger taken. He commented, "Whoever taped your finger at the football game did a great job!" Mom and Dad were proud to see John working as an EMT on the sidelines of the Grafton High School football games.

During the 1970s, John worked part time as a dispatcher at the Grafton Police Department on Providence Road in Grafton, Massachusetts. He was trained by Cathy Fenton, one of the first "unofficial" female police officers in the town of Grafton. John enjoyed doing police dispatching and bought our mother a police scanner so she could listen to him at home. The whole family enjoyed listening to the police scanner and hearing the local police activity.

Cathy Fenton
Dispatcher at Grafton
Police Station.

John attended the University of Hawaii during the spring semester in 1980. He enjoyed taking college classes that interested him. It did not matter whether the classes were associated with a particular degree or program. In addition, he took classes at Holyoke Community College, Worcester State College, Quinsigamond Community College, and Northeastern University in Boston, Massachusetts.

John attended the Amity Aero Tech Institute and earned his Private Pilot License on January 23, 1984. He flew over the town of Grafton on multiple occasions, taking photographs of the town from his plane. One of his pictures was included in the 1985 Town of Grafton Calendar.

John completed the Emergency Medical Technician Paramedic Program at Northeastern University on February 2, 1986. He began a new career working at U-Mass Hospital in Worcester, Massachusetts, as a Life Flight helicopter dispatcher. A few times he was called upon to accompany the crew on the helicopter as an additional EMT and paramedic.

John Jr. – Dispatcher for Life Flight UMass Hospital

JOHN NORMAN JR. OUELLETTE

John was involved in the formation of our band, *Slant 6 and the Jumpstarts*. On Saturday mornings throughout the early to mid-1980s, Mom and Dad would go out for breakfast and food shopping at Stop & Shop in Westborough, Massachusetts. This was the only time we could get together and perform "live" jam sessions in our basement. John was our audio and video engineer. He recorded many of our practices on cassettes and videotaped many of these early sessions.

John passed away at the Halifax Medical Center in Daytona Beach, Florida, on April 1, 1996, after a long illness. John was an inspiration and a role model. Imagine a world with more people like John.

CHAPTER 21

James Andrew Ouellette

The term "Irish twins" refers to two children born to the same mother within twelve months of each other. The term originated in the 1800s to make fun of Irish Catholic immigrant families who did not have access to or chose not to use birth control. Jim and I are Irish twins.

James (Jim) Baptism 1957 – Monterey, CA

James Andrew Ouellette was born on March 25, 1957, at Monterey Hospital in Monterey, California and was baptized about two weeks later. Dad was attending the US Army Language School in Monterey, learning to speak Romanian. According to J. Edgar Hoover, there needed to be at least one or two agents at any time who could speak an existing foreign language for interrogation purposes. At the time, they were living at 195 Cedar Street in Pacific Grove, California.

Jim remembers living on 115th Street in Cleveland, Ohio, and then at the duplex at 1371 Thoreau Road in Lakewood, Ohio. He attended kindergarten at Garfield Elementary School and was in the same class as

Sherry Weber, who lived next door in the duplex on Thoreau Road. Sherry is the daughter of Mr. Weber, an FBI agent stationed with Dad at the Cleveland Office. Mr. and Mrs. Weber had another daughter named Dawn, who was John's age. As previously mentioned, John and Jim would talk to Sherry and Dawn between the unfinished wall separating the attics of the duplex. They talked about safety school, a program that taught young children how to safely walk along and cross streets and navigate intersections.

Jim's 1st Birthday
3-25-1958

Jim attended St. Rose Catholic School in early elementary school. I remember an incident while walking home from St. Rose with John and Jim when we came upon a young boy from our school who had been hit by a large semi-truck and pinned under the wheel. We stopped and stared in shock as this young boy from our school stared upward while a priest knelt next to him, providing last rites.

As we continued to walk home, Jim told me that if the boy died, he would go straight to heaven because he had been baptized. I remember thinking to myself that I was lucky to have been baptized and, for the first time, realized how quickly our lives can end, regardless of age. This was my first encounter with mortality. The next day, upon arriving at school, we were brought to the church to pray for his recovery. Amazingly, the boy survived and was told he would not be able to walk again until he was eighteen years old. This might have been because the surgeries he required could not take place until he had completed most of his physical growth.

The first car Dad had owned as an FBI agent was a 1952 Plymouth he purchased while stationed in Detroit, Michigan. This was the last year Plymouth automobiles were manufactured with split windshields. By 1955, most automobile manufacturers had phased out split windshields.

Jim remembers how the back window of the 1952 Plymouth curved down to a shelf and that if you were small enough, you could crawl into this area and look out the back. Jim described to me how the car door panel had extra room and that if the door was accidentally closed on a person's fingers, they would not be hurt. This happened to Jim, and his fingers were not injured.

During heavy snowfall, Dad attached chains to the tires for better traction. He always had to do this during a major snowfall or blizzard. Once the roads were plowed, the chains had to be removed, which was a frustrating task for him because it totally disrupted his day. Dad was glad when snow tires were invented.

While living on Thoreau Road, Dad and Jim walked up the street to an automobile dealership to check out the cars. Dad had mentioned that it was time to buy a new vehicle. Jim noticed a 1960 Mercury Monterey sitting on the lot and told Dad he should buy it. It is possible that Jim liked the name of the car because he was born in Monterey, California. Dad bought the car.

Jim enjoyed the many activities Dad planned for us on the weekends during the 1960s. This was a great way to keep us older children, John, Jim, Mark, and Paul, active while Mom stayed home with Marie, Neal and eventually Rich.

Playing kick the can was a fun game. Jim was fast for his age and did well. During nice weather, Dad took us outside after dinner and played with us until it became dark. If you were ever caught and standing in the kick the can "jail," you could count on Jim to outrun the "searcher" and kick the can, allowing you to get out of jail. If Jim was the game's "searcher," you were in big trouble.

Jim remembers many of the get-togethers with other FBI agents and their families. He had a great time when we went to Euclid Beach and Cedar Point Amusement Parks.

There was a weekend when Dad took us on a day trip to Huntington Beach Park in Cleveland, where Jim discovered a large patch of four-leaf clovers. To find so many four-leaf clovers in a patch together is rare. We returned to the park a few weeks later and tried to help him find this magical discovery, but we were unsuccessful. The memory of this great discovery is still with us.

Jim enjoyed going to "Wiggly Hills" and sliding down the smooth grass terraces on pieces of cardboard. He would run up and slide down those terraces faster than anyone else who was there. There was a statue of a bunny at the entrance of this park, which we called "The Easter Bunny." As simple as it was, this place was one where Jim's athletic abilities emerged and was a place of amazing childhood memories with our dad.

Jim was an excellent swimmer and never tired out when Dad took us to the Avon Lake Public Pool. He did forward and backward flips off the high diving board. I was terrified of the high diving board and found it challenging just to jump off feet first.

Jim was excited when Dad took us to the movie theater. He remembers going to see *The Sound of Music, Mary Poppins, The Blue Max, The Night They Raided Minsky's* and many of the James Bond films released in the 1960s. Dad bought the soundtrack to the James Bond movie *Thunderball.* Jim enjoyed listening to the record at home. He recalls being scared while watching *House on Haunted Hill* and *The Tingler* at the movie theater. He became so scared while watching *The Tingler* that he lifted his feet up off the floor of the theater in fear of a "tingler" crawling up his leg. Jim enjoyed listening to the soundtrack record albums of certain movies he saw at the theater. I remember how much he enjoyed listening to the soundtracks of the movies *Butch Cassidy & the Sundance Kid* and *Yellow Submarine.*

Every so often, Dad took us to the FBI Headquarters in Cleveland on a Saturday. On one occasion, Dad allowed Jim to bring his friend Paul Negulescu. Jim bought a poster to hang on his bedroom wall and was carrying it around in a tube-shaped paper bag. Jim and Paul Negulescu were confronted by the Police who searched Jim's bag only to find the poster. Someone had been walking around the city that day, smashing things with a metal pipe. The police thought Jim might be the culprit and was hiding a pipe in the poster bag. Imagine the policemen's reaction after Jim told them that his father worked for the FBI.

Dad took us on a day trip to Serpent Mound in Peebles, Ohio, in the late 1960s. Serpent Mound is an Indian burial mound and a historic landmark. Jim's friend Paul Negulescu was with us. Dad liked Paul and his family. Jim continues to stay in touch with Paul and his family. I also stay in touch with him and enjoy hearing the stories about the things he and Jim did together in Avon Lake.

James 1st Communion
Avon Lake, OH

Jim has always been a devoted Catholic. Even at an early age, I could ask him questions about the meaning and purpose of certain rituals and sacraments associated with the church. He was happy and proud after making his first communion. Dad brought him to the Aqua Marine Restaurant for breakfast to celebrate. This picture of Jim standing in front of our home in Avon Lake holding a Bible after his first communion is in a book about the history of Avon Lake published by Arcadia Book Company.

Jim became interested in radio at a young age. He followed and listened to many of the local radio stations and became familiar with the names of disc jockeys in the Cleveland area. Anytime we were going somewhere in our car, John and Jim asked Dad to put the radio on WIXY 1260, a new and popular radio station.

It's interesting to point out that in December 1965, WDOK-AM became WIXY 1260 and was one of the first radio stations to feature high-energy disc jockey personalities offering contests and prizes to listeners. WIXY 1260 brought the Beatles to Cleveland.

Jim liked to make cassette tapes featuring himself as a disc jockey. He would talk about and play his favorite songs and often include funny stories and skits with sound effects. Sometimes, he gave or sent these cassettes to friends and relatives.

Jim enjoyed listening to the ham radio that he and John shared in their bedroom. I learned a lot about ham radios from Jim over the years. It was interesting listening to people talk to each other, even when they spoke a foreign language that we could not understand. I recall a few occasions when we guessed what language they were speaking or what country they were transmitting from. It was interesting listening to the Morse code transmissions. I learned basic Morse code as a Cub Scout but had a difficult time following these live transmissions because they were too fast.

Jim was the most energetic participant in our backyard activities during the 1960s. He was someone you wanted on your team when an "apple war" was being organized. As previously mentioned, "apple wars" was a neighborhood game that took place in the small apple orchard behind our house. We divided ourselves into two teams and threw apples at each other. This lasted until someone was injured, and our mother would come outside to end the game. Jim was the first to sneak a firecracker into an apple and light it before throwing. These exploding apples made an awful sticky mess.

Jim enjoyed Halloween and loved carving pumpkins. He shared his love for carving pumpkins with our niece Elisa, my daughter Sarah, and later with Neal's children, John and Julia. There was nothing better than a Halloween carved pumpkin sitting on the steps of 5 Virginia Circle in Grafton.

During the 1960s, Jim was involved with converting our barn into a walk-through haunted attraction. He looked forward to the cool fall evenings when Dad took us out to the barn carrying a carved pumpkin with a lit candle to tell us ghost stories.

In the 1960s, we played touch football in the field behind our house in Avon Lake and then the side yard next to our home in Lorton, Virginia. I remember how fast Jim was and his ability to dodge defensive players. I could never tackle Jim, but remember Paul being fast enough to be able to sprint up and run side by side with Jim, making silly faces.

Jim was a natural-born explorer and adventurer. He never hesitated to head out with friends or on his own to explore. I remember one cold winter day when he discovered that the Avon Lake water tower had exploded, creating a mountain of ice. He was so excited when he returned home to tell us about his discovery. I immediately went back with him to see the spectacle and join in the fun. Kids were climbing to the top of the ice mountain and sliding down on their butts. The next day, Mom let Jim bring Neal, who was three or four years old, back to the water tower to slide. Neal did not like being there, so Jim walked him home. The water tower event lasted a few days until the Avon Lake Public Works Department closed off the area and cleaned up the mess, ending our fun.

Exploring French Creek was fun. The only concern would be slipping into the water with one or both of your feet and getting a "soaker." "Soakers" were not pleasant and could be extremely uncomfortable, especially in the winter. In the summer, we liked to catch crawfish with nets in the creek. Crawfish were excellent bait for fishing in Lake Erie.

Jim and John both enjoyed the television culture that was evolving in the Cleveland area during the 1960s. As young children, we liked to watch *Romper Room* hosted by Barbara Plummer, known as Miss Barbara, on WEWS Channel 5. *Romper Room* was an American children's series that was franchised and syndicated from 1953 to 1994 targeting children five years of age or younger.

Captain Penny, played by Ron Penfound, of *The Captain Penny Show*, was a children's show that featured *The Three Stooges, Little Rascals* and old cartoons. Captain Penny had special guest characters such as Jungle Larry, Franz the Toymaker and Woody Woodsmen, to name a few. Toward the mid and late 1960s, Jim and John were inspired and entertained by Cleveland television shows *The Hoolihan & Big Chuck Show*, Big Chuck and Lil' John, *Ghoulardi's "Shock Theater"* and *Super Host* played by Marty Sullivan.

It was in the late 1960s when a new apartment complex was being constructed in the large field behind our house in Avon Lake. I am not sure where Mom and Dad were, but I remember Jim walking over and getting in one of the large construction backhoe loaders, starting the engine and driving around the field. Jim was around twelve years old. I watched in "shock and awe" as he drove the vehicle in circles, purposely crashing into things. I guess the construction workers should not have left the keys in the ignition.

At age thirteen, Jim landed his first formal job at the coin-operated Avon Lake Car Wash, located a short distance from our house. He worked Saturdays earning one dollar per hour, making change for customers, adding powder soap to the machines and changing the trash bucket bags when full. While other employees did not like changing the paper vacuum bags customers filled while vacuuming the insides of their vehicles, Jim did not mind. He learned that people accidentally or unknowingly picked up coins and spare change while using these powerful vacuums.

Jim would remove the vacuum paper trash bags and sort through the dirt and dust to find coins. Sometimes he made more money finding coins in the vacuum bags than he made working a full Saturday shift. Jim told me that the owner of the car wash had him attach high-voltage warning plates to the coin boxes. While the coin boxes had nothing to do with high voltage, the owner wanted it done to deter people from trying to pry open the metal boxes and stealing the money.

Jim's friend Bill, also known as "King Willy," worked at the Avon Lake Laundry Mat next door to the car wash. After work, Jim and "King Willy" would go on what they called "espionage missions," where they explored open construction sites and abandoned houses in the area before going home.

Soon after moving to Grafton, Massachusetts, in April 1972, Jim met Arthur Corriveau. Arthur was a hardworking French Canadian who lived off Grafton Common and was known as a "Jack of all trades." Arthur was always looking to hire helpers and laborers for different jobs he was involved with in the area. These jobs included cutting and stacking wood, painting, digging, moving furniture, shoveling snow, and small demolitions, to name a few.

**Jim Early 1970s
Grafton, MA**

Arthur became a great friend and allowed us to hang out in his basement to play pool. He invited Jim to go hunting, fishing, camping, and apple picking with his family. Arthur was the kind of person who would help anyone at any time. In the early 1980s, Jim wrote a song for our band, *Slant 6 and the Jumpstarts,* honoring Arthur. The name of the song is "Arthur."

When I was a freshman and Jim a junior at Grafton High School, our parents went away for the day. While they were gone, we had a small party at the house. During the party, someone lit and flushed an M80 explosive down the toilet and blew it into pieces. Jim called Arthur, who arrived at our house about an hour later with tools and a new toilet. He replaced the toilet and was gone before Mom and Dad returned home.

Jim as Senior
Grafton HS Football 1974

While attending Grafton High School, Jim participated in cross-country and track and field. He played football in his senior year.

There were special places in Grafton that were designated as places to meet and hang out during the 1970s and 1980s. Browns Road was one of those popular locations and a great place to socialize.

Jim had become good friends with the Pease family on Old Upton Road in the early 1970s. He would house-sit for the family when they went on vacation or traveled with Mr. Pease on business. Jim also became friends with Mr. and Mrs. Pease's son Jamie and daughter Christy.

I knew Christy from school and would see her at Norcross Park on North Street while playing basketball. Christy was friends with Sue and Lynne Dayutis, who lived in a house next to Norcross Park. I have some great memories of hanging out with Christy, Sue, and Lynne in the early 1970s. Occasionally, Jim took me along when he wanted to stop by and say hello to the Pease family. This was how I first met Mr. and Mrs. Pease and Jamie.

Jim & Jack Chartier

The Pease family owned a large parcel of land that surrounded the railroad tracks on Browns Road. The Peases told Jim that he and his friends could hang out there any time, and if we were over eight feet from the railroad tracks, we were on the Pease's private land. This became quite the party spot. In the mid-1980s, our band, *Slant 6 and the Jumpstarts,* recorded and released our first album, *Browns Road.*

Jim made some great friends soon after we moved to Grafton. He quickly became friends with Ken Holland and Jack Chartier, who both lived in our neighborhood.

Jim and his friends developed another popular gathering location in the parking lot in front of the Grafton Credit Union in North Grafton, referred to as "The Lot." It was an excellent location, with high visibility, where anyone who was driving by could stop and hang out on Saturday afternoons after the bank closed. This was a place where discussions would take place as to potential Saturday night activities.

Charlie Bolack, owner of the Grafton Credit Union, gave permission to Jim and any of his friends to park their cars in front of the building on the condition that they were orderly and respectful. Jim and his friends enjoyed this tradition throughout the 1980s and mid-1990s.

Jim attended Quinsigamond Community College in Worcester, Massachusetts, after graduating from Grafton High School in 1975. He attended the college part time over a five-year period while working a variety of full and part-time jobs. Jim later graduated from Quinsigamond Community College with an Associate Degree in Liberal Arts in 1980.

Slant 6 and the Jumpstarts

He continued his part-time college career, attending Worcester State College and earning his bachelor's degree in English in 1985. Jim qualified to become a member of the Mensa High IQ Society. To qualify, a person must score in the 98th percentile (top 2 percent) or higher on a standardized, supervised IQ test.

Jim was and still is the backbone of our band, *Slant 6 and the Jumpstarts*. He was blessed with the ability to create original and parody songs loaded with humor and satire. His ability to integrate humor and satire while performing live on stage was crucial to our band's success.

Jim worked a variety of interesting jobs during the 1980s. He was employed by Raytheon as a security guard, United Parcel Service, David Clark Company, Data General, Mayflower Moving Company and the Opportunities Industrial Center (O.I.C.), to name a few. Some of these jobs came to be while working with Suburban Temporary Service out of Westborough, Massachusetts.

Jim took a one-year break in 1985 and traveled to Knome, Alaska, to serve as a disc jockey and manager/director of radio station KNOM. The Jesuit Volunteer Corps operated the radio station. Jim enjoyed playing music, making public service announcements, and updating the bush pilot's schedules. Bush pilots were an important means of transportation in Alaska. They flew small planes to the many different villages, towns, and cities in Alaska.

Jim remembers covering the Iditarod Trail Sled Dog Race while in Alaska and having bush pilots fly him from village to village interviewing "mushers" in March 1986. The race ends in Knome, Alaska. I remember seeing the coverage of the race on the news. We tried to see if we could find Jim standing somewhere in the crowd. Mom thought she spotted him during the report.

After Jim returned from Alaska, our band was back in action, picking up where we left off the previous year. We recorded more albums and continued to perform live. It was amazing to hear our songs being played on radio stations.

Jim, Dr. Demento, Mark receive award from Dr. Demento in Boston, MA

We received documented verification from radio stations around the world that were playing our music. Jim's unique voice and clever lyrics were well received by college and FM radio stations. I remember running down North Street in Grafton, listening to our first 45 rpm release, "Pull the Plug," on WAAF on my portable Walkman radio. *Slant 6 and the Jumpstarts* had over forty of our songs played on the syndicated radio program, *The Dr. Demento Show*. Jim and I met Dr. Demento while he was in Boston at Tower Records in the 1990s after our song "Mrs. Fletcher (Help Me I've Fallen)" made it to number one for two weeks and number twenty on his top 100 songs of the year.

I recently asked Jim if he would tell me more about the jobs he had after graduating from high school. He said that during his career; he held multiple jobs and interacted with many interesting people. There was one particular year when Jim held eleven different jobs while signed up with Suburban Temporary Services.

I worked with Jim as an on-call spare at Mayflower Moving Company during the early and mid-1980s. Eventually, our brothers, Neal and Rich, also worked part time at the moving company. We did many moving jobs together, worked hard and had plenty of fun. I remember the dispatcher at Mayflower telling us that the Ouellette boys were at the top of the Mayflower "high demand" workers list.

In the late 1980s, Jim and I both worked for the Opportunities Industrial Center, headquartered on Main Street in Worcester, Massachusetts. I taught adult literacy classes at the Worcester office, while Jim taught adult education at the Great Brook Valley Branch. One day we were all called in to the main office in Worcester by the director and informed that the program was closing. He then invited the entire staff and office personnel to head over to the unemployment office and complete the paperwork required to collect unemployment checks. After completing the unemployment paperwork, we were all invited to Tweed's Restaurant to celebrate.

Jim and I looked at each other and politely declined the invitation, telling the director that we were not interested in collecting unemployment and would be going to work at the Mayflower Moving Company the next day. Jim and I were proud of not having taken advantage of the unemployment system and were the only ones in the company not to apply for unemployment and accept the invitation to celebrate at Tweed's Restaurant.

While Jim enjoyed hanging out and doing things with his friends, he also designated some Saturday nights as "date night." He had some nice girlfriends and was exceptionally polite and respectful to the girls he dated. There were a few occasions when Jim and I took our girlfriends out on a double date. My favorite double date was when we took the girls to the abandoned Grafton State Hospital and listened to the radio. There were a few occasions when we took our dates to the Edgemere Drive-In Theater. I remember watching *The Texas Chainsaw Massacre,* and the girls covered their eyes throughout the entire movie.

Jim remembers Dad telling him about an incident that took place while working at the FBI Headquarters in Washington, DC. Hoover, being a perfectionist, wanted memos and documents formatted correctly. He did not like seeing documents with any letters or words that extended into the margins or borders of the paper.

On one occasion, Hoover received a document with words extending into the border of the paper. He immediately sent out a memo to every agent in the country stating, "Watch the borders!" The agents understood this to mean they should be on high alert along the borders of the United States and state borders. Agents around the country quickly "scrambled" and positioned themselves at strategic border locations. Eventually, Hoover discovered what had happened and sent out another memo correcting the situation. Jim told me that Dad enjoyed telling him this story and thought it was funny.

Prior to his retirement in the 2010s, Jim worked as a substitute teacher at Grafton High School and Uxbridge High School. He continues to write music and contribute to our band, Slant 6 and the Jumpstarts. I know Jim could write an amazing book focusing on his life experiences. He once told me he had done so much in such a short time that he has already lived two lifetimes. I disagree and say it's more like three or four lifetimes

.

CHAPTER 22

Mark Stephen Ouellette

My earliest memory is of sitting in a high chair wearing a bib and being fed small pieces of barbecue ribs. Mom put the meat she had cut into small pieces on the tray in front of me. I believe I was around a year old.

There were concerns regarding my health and the potential of birth defects due to Mom having just gotten over German measles. I was born on March 1,1958 at 5:13 a.m. at Fairview Park Hospital in Cleveland, Ohio. A few weeks later, on March 23rd,1958, I was baptized at St. Bridget of Kildare Parish in Parma, Ohio. We lived in a small apartment in Parma and soon after my birth, moved to 115th Street in Cleveland.

L-R John Jr., Mark, Jim
1959 Cleveland, OH

I clearly remember running out the front door of our home on 115th Street, at around age two, and trying to get to the street. Our neighbor, Mrs. Lunic, an elderly Polish woman, rescued me. Mrs. Lunic lived next door and introduced us to pierogies, a potato and cheese filled dumpling.

Dad would set up a cardboard fireplace a few weeks before Christmas at our home on 115th Street. This house did not have a real fireplace. He set up the same cardboard fireplace at the duplex we later moved to on Thoreau Road.

While living on Thoreau Road, I used to sneak up the stairs to the attic and explore. On one occasion, I found some small, pointed plastic cups all over the floor. The pointed cups reminded me of a woodpecker. The *Woodie Woodpecker Show* was a popular television show, and I told Mom and Dad that a woodpecker lived in our attic. That must have raised a few red flags. Many years later, I talked with Mom about the "woodpecker" in the attic and, for the first time, she understood the situation. We laughed for some time and never brought it up again.

When I was in first grade, I wandered outside and stood on the sidewalk in front of our house. A young boy named David, who lived across the street, came outside and stabbed me at the base of my thumb with a jackknife. I ran inside our house crying and had to go to the hospital to get stitches. To this day, I have no idea why he did this.

I must have driven Mom and Dad crazy with my accidents and injuries at such an early age. There was an incident when I went up into the attic to explore and stepped on a rusty nail. As soon as Dad got home from work, he had to take me to the hospital for a tetanus shot before dinner. On the ride home from the hospital, Dad stopped for cigarettes and bought me a Pay Day candy bar.

The injuries continued when one afternoon I ran into a door on the first floor of our house and split my forehead open. Dad took me to the hospital, where I received stitches. After returning home from the hospital, John Jr. asked me what happened. I demonstrated what had happened and ran into the same door, splitting the same cut open again. I had to go back to the hospital to get new stitches.

I attended kindergarten at Garfield Elementary School in September 1963. Mom walked me to school on my first day. On the way, we delivered John and Jim to St. Rose Elementary School. A few months later, John and Jim came over to my school to walk me home after President Kennedy had been assassinated. The principal at my school came into my classroom and told us that the president had been shot, and we were to go home and pray. I stood by the main entrance of the school and waited for John and Jim to arrive, and we walked home together. The people we passed along the street were crying or praying out loud. I will never forget that day.

While attending kindergarten and first grade, I enjoyed drawing pictures relating to holidays and special events we celebrated as a family. My favorite drawings were those relating to Christmas, Thanksgiving, and Halloween. In school, we would draw Thanksgiving turkeys using our hands as an outline. We created colorful Christmas cards to bring home. The teachers would bring homemade cupcakes or cookies for the students to enjoy before Christmas vacation.

It was fun learning how to read. I learned the alphabet quickly and liked how it was presented as a song we would sing in class. We used phonics-based instruction along with the traditional Dick & Jane "whole word" reading method.

Second grade was a challenge. It was not because I was dumb that I failed second grade, but because I was afraid. The nun who served as my primary teacher was a severe disciplinarian. She would slam our knuckles with a ruler if we misspelled a word or made grammatical errors. If she thought we were not paying attention, she pinched and pulled our ears. If a student misbehaved or lied, she ordered the student to lean over the teacher's desk and then paddled them in front of the class.

After the paddling, you were directed to stand in the corner and pray for ten minutes. I never received a paddling but regularly went to school worrying about the possibility. I witnessed a few classmates being paddled, which horrified me. I could not focus or learn and began to fail all my subjects. My knuckles and ears took a beating that year. After it was decided that I would repeat the second grade, Mom and Dad decided to move to Avon Lake, Ohio. They pulled us out of the Catholic schools and enrolled us in the Avon Lake Public Schools.

I enjoyed attending Westview Elementary School in Avon Lake and did well in class. It was fun being able to buy school lunches. The lunch ladies sold chocolate raisin clusters for five cents after regular lunch was served. I loved those chocolate raisin clusters and was inspired to buy chocolate-covered raisins. Whenever we went to a movie theater, I bought a box of Raisinets. The opportunity to buy a school lunch made mornings much easier for Mom. It was much more convenient to hand each of us a few coins than to prepare a bag lunch every morning.

In the spring of 1966, Mom took the training wheels off my bike and coached me to ride using momentum and balance. On my ninth birthday in 1967, I received a new bike with high handlebars and a banana seat. I rode that bike all over town and could "pop-a-wheely" over long distances for as long as I desired. I liked to ride my bike northward up to the end of our street and walk around the Avon Lake Marina. It was fun watching the boats come in and out while looking at the different size minnows that were kept in large tanks. Fishermen bought the minnows to use as bait.

On pleasant afternoons, I rode my bike up the street to my school, Westview Elementary, to see if there were any kickball games being played. Kickball was the most popular game at my school. It was one of the few games that allowed both boys and girls to play together.

For safety reasons, the school disallowed students from biking to and from school. Westview Elementary School was only a few hundred yards up the street, providing a convenient commute. I remember walking to school and then running home as fast as possible to watch the new television show *Dark Shadows* with Mom. Mom usually prepared boiled hotdogs on a bun or a can of Campbell's Chicken Noodle Soup for my after-school snack because dinner wasn't served until around 6:30 or 7:00 p.m.

While on vacation in Florida during the summer of 1968, I became ill and had to spend time in the hospital. While doctors could not determine what was wrong with me, I was nauseous, dizzy and not able to eat anything. I was ten years old. On the second day, I developed a high fever and could not move. According to my medical records, my heart stopped beating, and the doctor, along with two nurses, came into my room to perform CPR.

L – R Mark, Paul, John, Jim & Marie with Carrier Pigeon Avon Lake, Ohio 1965

While all of this was going on, I floated out of my body and watched from above. I felt fantastic and wanted to tell everyone in the room that I was fine. I felt physically solid and complete and did not feel sick anymore. Navigating myself to a standing position next to my bed, I noticed a bright light in the distance coming toward me and expanding.

It was a large, bright, circular opening to a beautiful place with lots of people. I wanted to step inside the entrance and learn more, but a voice said, "Not yet!"

While standing next to this entrance, I was able to briefly meet and communicate with four people I had never met before and one I had known briefly. For personal reasons, I will not identify who these people were or what they said to me, but I will share that they were happy and excited to see me. I could see more people approaching me as I stood at the edge of this entrance but felt myself being pulled back toward my body. Next, I re-entered my body, which felt like a quick electrical shock, and looked around at everyone standing around me. I felt sick again and wished I could go back.

Prior to being discharged from the hospital, I shared the details of my conversations with the people I met with Dad and the doctor. I was told that what happened to me was personal and private and should not be discussed with anyone.

I am fortunate to have had this experience and look forward to finding out what it is like being inside that bright light. This was the most powerful and emotional experience I have ever encountered.

Sitting down and looking through the Sears and JC Penney catalogs that came in the mail before Christmas was fun. Circling certain items that I hoped to get for Christmas was something I looked forward to, and it built my excitement for the holidays.

Christmas 1968 was truly memorable. I received a single pump-action Daisy BB rifle with a tube-fed loader. I spent hours target practicing, shooting at FBI-issued paper targets and tin cans. With my BB gun in tow, I hiked up and down French Creek for hours at a time, regardless of the weather or time of year. I could hold my BB gun behind my back and hit a tin can twenty yards away.

Mark, CEI Building, Avon Lake, Ohio 2015

Lake Erie was a great place for boating and fishing. I remember our teachers telling us never to walk out on the lake when it froze in the winter. The fresh water quickly froze and created what we referred to as "mountains of ice." A person could walk on three feet of ice and then suddenly step where there is less than an inch of ice and plummet into the freezing water. It seemed that every year one or two kids from our area drowned because of attempting to walk on the thin ice.

The CEI Building in Avon Lake was a dreary-looking structure built on the shore of Lake Erie in the 1920s. The building was owned and operated by the Cleveland Electric Company. Behind the building was an area referred to as "The Cut." This was where water was drawn inside to cool the machinery that made electricity. According to legend and folklore, a person who swam too close to "The Cut" would be sucked in and chopped to pieces. I still fear "The Cut."

Mom and Dad convinced me to join the Cub Scouts. I liked wearing my uniform and enjoyed the patriotism associated with being a Cub Scout. I never advanced to Boy Scouts but was allowed to go on a camping trip and canoe adventure with John and Jim and their Boy Scout Troop.

Any time I wanted a treat, it was only a short and quick bike ride to Lawson's or the Ben Franklin Store at the small plaza across the street from the lake. Everyone enjoyed the orange "Wowee Wax Whistles" that were sold for five cents prior to Halloween. These whistles consisted

Halloween Wax Whistle

of a dull, orange-flavored chewing wax. We would buy these whistles and climb up and hang on to the limbs of a tree next to French Creek, swaying back and forth while blowing on the whistles. We called it "The Poor People's Tree." I think the shape and size of the tree somehow made us think that even poor people could afford such a tree.

SKY BAR

Candy bars were only five cents back in the early to mid-1960s. Pay Day candy bars were my favorite. If I did not have any money, I rode my bike up and down the street searching for discarded bottles I could turn in at Lawson's Store for two cents apiece. My favorite candy bar was Pay Day. I would eat a Pay Day candy bar by first nibbling on the peanuts on the exterior of the bar and then delving into the interior when I could no longer resist the temptation. On one occasion, Jim and I were at the corner drugstore at the plaza, and Jim convinced me to buy a Sky Bar. He told me it was like having a milk chocolate bar with four different fillings. It was delicious, and I still buy a Sky Bar every so often.

I had no trouble finding things to do in Avon Lake and never got bored. I recall riding my bike up to the plaza where the Saddle Inn Restaurant was located. As I pedaled into the parking lot, I saw my dad and about eight other men standing around a car with a man handcuffed, sitting in the backseat. Dad called me over and introduced me to the other agents and with a smile told me they had just arrested a Russian spy. I went home so excited and told Mom what had happened.

I enjoyed getting on my bike and riding around town. Sometimes I grabbed my BB gun and hiked up and down French Creek for hours at a time. If I were tired, I walked over to the apple orchard and checked on the apple crop. If John and Jim were doing something together, I could play with Paul, Marie, and Neal, or watch Rich trying to escape from his crib.

As previously mentioned, the Allied Moving Company truck arrived at our house in Avon Lake a few days after Christmas Day in 1970. The last item to go on the truck was our Christmas tree. A few days later, we arrived at our new home on Ox Road in Lorton, Virginia. When the movers were done unloading the truck, Dad set up the Christmas tree and took Mom to the Super Giant Grocery Store in Woodbridge, Virginia.

The house in Lorton, Virginia, a beautiful red brick structure, provided us with plenty of space for our large family. John had received the new Beatles album *Let It Be* and played it over and over on the stereo record player that was set up in the living room. Dad played Guy Lombardo records on New Year's Eve and enjoyed watching the college football games. Dad had taken a full week off for the transition, and we had a great time settling in and exploring the area. On New Year's Eve, our neighbors, Mr. and Mrs. Carlson, came over to introduce themselves. Mrs. Carlson brought us homemade peanut butter potato candy as a welcome gift. I had never had it before and loved it. Mrs. Carlson gave Mom the recipe. It is made with sweetened white potato dough that is rolled out like a pizza. Peanut butter is spread across the surface of the dough and then rolled up, taking on the shape of a tube or pipe. Powdered sugar is sprinkled on the exterior and then placed in the freezer. It is meant to be eaten cold or frozen.

Living in Lorton was a wonderful adventure. I attended Lorton Elementary School for the second half of the sixth grade. I remember being disappointed that nobody played or organized kickball games during recess. Whenever we went outside for recess, everyone walked around looking at each other, waiting for something to happen. This one "tough" girl that everyone feared would walk around trying to get people to sing John Lennon's "Power to the People." When she looked at me, I pretended to be singing.

I attended the first half of seventh grade at Washington Irving Intermediate Junior High School in Springfield, Virginia. It was an unfamiliar experience, and for the first time, I traveled to different classes on a specific academic schedule. It was a long bus ride to and from this school, and sometimes I fell asleep. There was a jukebox in the cafeteria, and students could play songs during lunch. I remember hearing "If Not for You" performed by Olivia Newton-John, "The Night They Drove Old Dixie Down," performed by Joan Baez and "Just Another Day" written and sung by Paul McCartney being played repeatedly.

Living close to the Alcohol Rehabilitation Center offered some interesting opportunities. We could walk there at night and buy candy and soda from the outdoor vending machines. Jeff, a friend of ours who lived up the street, would take us into the tunnel system that was built under the complex. Jeff was not the best influence.

There were no fences or walls surrounding the facility. There were guard towers with spotlights, making sure patients did not walk or run away. It was supposed to be a new form of rehabilitation for people who committed crimes while under the influence of alcohol or drugs. I don't think Mom and Dad knew, but we sometimes snuck up and attempted to get to the base of the towers without being seen by the guards. We never got caught.

There was a Nike Missile Defense complex near our house. This was a facility with defensive missiles to protect Washington, DC, from nuclear attack. I would ride my bike to the perimeter of the Nike Site and hide behind trees, attempting to watch the missiles when they came out of the ground during maintenance checks on Saturday mornings at 10:00 a.m.. Security guards detained you if you were spotted watching from a distance.

Soon after settling into our new home in Lorton, Dad brought us to the Catholic Church in Woodbridge to sign up as members. The priest seemed in a hurry and asked if I had been confirmed. I told him I had not. He asked if I had a white shirt and tie; I told him I did. He then informed us that if I could go home and change clothes and be back quickly, I could be confirmed. Jim was on hand to be my "sponsor." The priest confirmed me that evening without having to attend any CCD classes.

I had fun riding my bike to Occoquan Village, about a mile and a half down the road. It was a steep downhill ride, and a person on a bike never needed to pedal to get there. Coming home was a long uphill battle. I recall one hot July day when I rode my bike to Occoquan and went to the General Store. I bought an ice-cold 16 oz. Royal Crown Cola and sat on my bike at the base of the one-lane Occoquan River bridge, sipping the cola for about twenty minutes before returning home.

I built an amazing one-room cabin in the woods behind our house in Lorton. After cutting down one-inch straight trees, I tied the sticks together with thick brown thread. I was inspired by the tiki huts that were built for the TV set of *Gilligan's Island*. While working on my secret one-room cabin, I noticed broken bottles and glass next to the stone wall separating our backyard from the farmland next to us. I dug with a stick and uncovered old bottles. My favorite is a White House Vinegar bottle dating back to the early 1900s. I found about twenty unbroken bottles. Mom and Dad told me they could be worth money. I brought the bottles with me when we moved to Grafton, Massachusetts, where I continued to "bottle hunt."

Moving to Grafton, Massachusetts, in April 1972 was exciting. Soon after moving into our home at 5 Virginia Circle, I made friends with Ken Holland, Doug Walsh, and Jim Chartier. We used to get together with our BB guns and explore the woods behind our house. I was able to convince my new friends to assist me in searching for antique bottles. We learned that people dumped their trash somewhere on their property before public and town trash removal existed. We found many old bottles behind old stone walls in the woods and fields behind historic homes in town. I have never sold any of my bottles and now have over 800 in my collection.

I attended Grafton Middle School for the last two months of seventh grade. Ken Holland, Jim Chartier, Doug Walsh, and I walked to school together. On my first day at Grafton Middle School, I was walking out of the cafeteria with my lunch tray when a student, Richard Whitney, invited me to sit at his table. After lunch, we were allowed to stand outside the cafeteria and socialize with other students. A few students were throwing pebbles at the roof of the house directly across the street. After a few minutes, a woman, Mrs. Harrington, walked over and told us, "If one more pebble hits the roof of my house, it will be the last thing you ever do." We never threw rocks at her roof again.

Ironically, during the summer of 1973, prior to entering ninth grade, I met and became friends with Mrs. Harrington's son John while playing basketball at Norcross School on North Street. John invited me down to his house to lift weights with his friend Paul three days a week after playing basketball at Norcross. I am not sure if Mrs. Harrington recognized me, but I was able to become good friends with the Harrington family.

Mr. and Mrs. Harrington have four children: Catherine, Linda, Patricia, and John. Mrs. Harrington made the best iced tea and always had a pitcher available while we lifted weights in the basement. It was during the summer of 1973 while playing basketball at Norcross Park on North Street when I met Sue Dayutis, Lynne Dayutis, and Christy Pease. On more than one occasion, my friends Ken Holland, Doug Walsh, and I camped out at the Norcross Park softball field and hung out with everyone listed above. While camping out, we made a bonfire and enjoyed talking and telling stories. There were a few times when we slept over at the old schoolhouse at Christy's house and told ghost stories throughout the night.

The summer of 1973 was a turning point in my life. Lifting weights, running and basketball became priorities. I attended Firearms Safety School and was given a Harrington & Richardson single-shot 20-gauge shotgun on my fifteenth birthday. I enjoyed hunting and target shooting. While following the rules and guidelines we learned at Gun Safety School, we would walk around Grafton Center with our unloaded shotguns like cowboys in the Wild West. I am not sure kids could get away with doing that today.

Ken Holland, Jim Chartier, and I built a one-room log cabin in the woods behind our house using old railroad ties. In nice weather, we would head out to the cabin after the Saturday 4:00 p.m. Mass with shotguns and spend the night in the cabin. We would sit on the roof of the cabin and shoot at cans. Dad brought me cases of shotgun shells from the FBI office in Boston. Staying up all night talking and laughing made the next morning quite challenging and I was thankful that I had already gone to Mass the day before.

During the summer of 1973, I was introduced to Arthur Corriveau, a talented French-Canadian lumberman who lived right off Grafton Common in Grafton Center. My brother Jim had already been working for Arthur as an on-call laborer. If Arthur needed a "helper" and Jim was not available, I filled in for him. We became great friends with Arthur and his wife, Claire. Their three children: Rene, Sonya, and Donald, were constantly running around playing in the yard when we worked on a project at their house.

On one occasion, Ken Holland and I were digging out Arthur's septic tank so he could make some modifications. Arthur told Sonya and Donald not to use or flush the toilet while we were in the septic hole. Arthur went out to buy some gravel and told us he would be back soon.

After about a minute or two, Ken and I heard a gushing sound, and before we could evacuate the hole, we had toilet water and poop all over our feet and legs. We looked up and could see Donald peeking out the bathroom window, laughing at us. Thankfully, when Sonya joined in on the fun, she just flushed the toilet and did not send any "special" packages. After Arthur returned, he looked at Ken and me as we continued to work in the hole and said, "Dirty stuff." I don't think we told him what Sonya and Donald had done.

Mark Grade 8

My plan was to run cross country as a freshman in high school, but John Harrington convinced me to play football. I had never played organized football but enjoyed the challenge. I played fullback and middle linebacker on the junior varsity team. My head was big and could only fit into an old 1950s helmet that provided little or no protection. I received two concussions in my freshman year and was told by my doctor to take two aspirins and rest a day or two, and then I could return to practice and games.

I played varsity football in my sophomore, junior, and senior years at Grafton High School. In my junior year, we received a special acknowledgement by Channel Five Sports as being the best backfield in New England. Steve LeMay was quarterback, John Harrington and Steve Kaczynski were at halfback, and I was at fullback.

Our varsity football team was undefeated in the regular season during my senior year in 1976. I was one of three captains of the football team. Jim Amaral and Mike Banks were the other captains. We played in the Super Bowl that year. I received the Most Valuable Player award but felt we should have received a "team" MVP Award. I enjoyed being a mentor and supporting the younger players.

Quarterback Steve LeMay #38 Handing Ball Off to Mark #31

It was during the 1976 Grafton High School football season that our quarterback, Steve Spagnuolo, led the team to the school's first undefeated regular season and trip to the Super Bowl. My dad had been filming the games so the coaches and players could review the films to help improve team play. We did not realize until the end of the season that he had documented one of the best football seasons in Grafton High School history.

My favorite memory of this season was when players Craig LeClaire, Mike Conway, Mike LeMay, and Steve Spagnuolo were walking back from the football field after a game, surrounded my dad while talking, smiling and laughing. Later that day, Dad told me how much he enjoyed talking to them and how friendly and respectful they were.

Grafton High School #17-Steve Spagnuolo
hands the ball off to #31-Mark Ouellette

Steve went on to enjoy a long career in professional football, winning multiple NFL Super Bowl titles and is currently the defensive head coach for the Kansas City Chiefs. Many believe he has already earned the honor of being the "Greatest NFL Defensive Coach" ever.

Basketball was my favorite sport. I would go to Norcross Park on North Street in the winter and shovel snow off the basketball court to practice. During my freshman year, I became one of the starting five on the freshman basketball team. The following year, I became one of two captains on the junior varsity team. In my junior and senior years, I played on the GHS Varsity Basketball Team. I received the Most Dedicated Player trophy my senior year. That award meant more to me than any other I had received while in high school.

In the spring of 1974, I joined the GHS track and field program. I ran the 400 and threw the discus. We could take part in two running events and two throwing events. As a result, I also ran the mile relay and threw the shot put. There were a few occasions when I helped the team by throwing the javelin or doing the high jump. I surpassed the GHS school discus record during the state competition in the spring of 1977.

While attending Grafton High School, I participated in football, basketball, and track all four years. During this time, I was able to meet and get to know some fantastic people. I learned that what I loved most was not the sport, but the conditioning and training associated with it. I became addicted to weightlifting and running.

**#17- Steve Spagnuolo,
#25- Mike Banks,
#31 Mark Ouellette**

My favorite high school memory was during the winter of 1975 when Ken Holland and I went to Washington, DC, on a weekend trip. Dad allowed me to take his Plymouth Valiant, "The Green Box," and handed me a credit card to pay for hotel rooms and gas. He told me that if there were any problems while in Washington, to call the FBI Headquarters and tell them my name and they would help. Dad still knew most of the agents stationed there and was well known.

During our trip, Ken and I visited Lorton, Virginia, and drove around Washington to see the monuments. We visited the Jefferson Memorial and explored the Smithsonian Museum. This trip to Washington DC was my first experience with being independent.

Attending Worcester Academy in the fall of 1977 as a postgraduate student was an excellent opportunity to improve my social and academic skills. While I felt a little awkward, I enjoyed the "Prep School" atmosphere and wearing a suit jacket and tie. If a student came to class without a tie, they were

Mark #31 – Mike Banks #25 – Super Bowl 1976

told they could not enter the room until they found one.

I played football at Worcester Academy and had an amazing pre-season. I ran for over 100 yards in each of our pre-season games. Unfortunately, on the first play of our first game of the season, I ran for a fifty-yard touchdown and tore my achilles tendon while entering the end zone.

Eventually, I returned from the injury late in the season but never fully recovered before the season ended.

The Blizzard of 1978 was fun. We would slide down Worcester Street on sleds all the way from Grafton Common to Fleming's Package Store next to Lake Ripple. Jim and I made good money working for Arthur Corriveau, shoveling snow off roofs in the area.

After attending college at the University of Massachusetts for a few weeks, I decided it was not the best program for me if I wanted to become a certified teacher. I packed my AMC Gremlin and headed back to Grafton. I took advantage of the fact that I was now living independently, sharing the

L – R Mark Ouellette, Jim Chartier,
Ken Holland - Early 1980s

house with John and Jim while the rest of the family was overseas. We had a former neighbor, Jim Dalton, also living at the house with us to "keep an eye" on things while everyone else was out of the country. Jim Dalton was a great guy and helped us when our cars broke down. We had some great parties at the house that fall.

I took a part-time job as a bouncer at the Red Barn Nightclub in Westboro, Massachusetts. The job was fun but somewhat dangerous when we had to deal with violent drunks. I ended up quitting when I became tired of dealing with the problems.

In 1977, I joined the Catalina Health Club in Shrewsbury, Massachusetts. I made some great friends while working out there. Billy, the owner, was an inspiration and constantly offered positive workout advice. Ken "Fishnet" Feldmen was quite the character. He would recruit any good-looking girls who happened to be working out at the gym to "spot" him while doing heavy lifts.

In 1979, I began participating in local road races. I ran the Charlie's 10 Mile Road Race, and later, The Grafton Gazebo Road Race, and the Whitinsville Turkey Trot, to name a few.

Mom, Paul, Marie, Neal, and Richard returned to Grafton a few weeks before Christmas in 1979. I remember Marie and I going out into the woods behind our house and cutting down a perfectly shaped pine "Christmas" tree. While the tree looked great, it dripped sap everywhere. It was the first and last time we ever cut down a wild pine tree to use as a Christmas tree.

Mark - Charlie's 10 Mile Road Race 1980s

On Christmas Eve 1979, my brother Jim, Ken Holland, Jack Chartier, Jim Chartier, and I went to the Grafton Inn to play pool and listen to the old jukebox. Prior to renovation, the inn was in rough shape. Later in the evening, we walked over to St. Philip's Parish for midnight Mass. Father Lounge was not happy watching us get up and down to use the bathroom throughout Mass. The following Saturday at evening Mass, he announced the bathroom would be locked during Mass.

It was in the fall of 1978 when I first began friendships with Laura Holland and her friend, Mary Sheehan. At the time I was attending Worcester Academy, they were students at Grafton High School. Most of

Mark – Grafton Inn 1979

my friends were away living at college, so it was nice having two new friends that enjoyed exploring the vacant Grafton State Hospital, hanging out at Browns Road, or sitting and talking at the Norcross School field on Worcester Street. It was in early 1980 when Mary and I began dating.

I first met Mary's mother, Mary Ann, and her husband, John Fargo, in early 1980. They lived in a house at the bottom of Oak Street, beside the Oak Street Cemetery. Over a short period, I became friends with Mary's sisters, Michelle and Moira, and their brother Mike, who they called "Secret Squirrel." I think it was because of the button-down, detective-style jacket he wore.

Mark with Mary Sheehan 1982

Eventually, I was invited to go out to dinner and attend special family events with Mary and her family. My parents liked Mary from the start and were thrilled to see us going to church together at St. Philip's. I remember how nice it felt when Mary's mother gave me the new Ringo Starr album, *Stop and Smell the Roses*, as a Christmas gift in 1980. I think of Mary Ann Fargo every time I see that album cover. Mary was a fantastic girlfriend, and we could talk for hours at a time or simply sit quietly and enjoy being together.

John & Mary Ann Fargo
Duck Island NC mid 1980s

While attending Worcester State College as an undergraduate, Mary finished high school and entered the St. Vincent Hospital Nursing School program in Worcester, Massachusetts. The nuns who ran the school were strict. Mary was an excellent student and received her nursing cap at the end of the two-year program.

I graduated from Worcester State College in 1984, earning a B.S. in Sociology and teaching certification in the Behavioral Sciences. Unfortunately, there were few teaching jobs available, so I entered the master's degree program at Worcester State College. Ironically, Mary entered the Bachelor Nursing Program at Worcester State College, and we both graduated together two years later.

Carol & Francis Sheehan

During those two years, Mary worked part time as a nurse while I worked part time for Mayflower Moving Company and the Budweiser Distribution Center in Auburn, Massachusetts, on Friday nights. During those two years, many of our dates were simply being together and studying. We found time to go to the movies, go out for dinner, attend parties with friends, and take weekend trips to Cape Cod, the White Mountains, and Maine.

We were married in February 1988 during a huge snowstorm. Bishop Reger conducted the service. Bishops rarely conduct weddings but agreed to do the ceremony because he was close friends with Mary's dad. We went to Europe on our honeymoon and visited England, France, Wales,

Switzerland, and Italy. It was more of an adventure than a romantic experience, yet we had a great time.

Mark Ouellette

After the honeymoon, I moved into the apartment Mary was renting on Jones Street in Worcester. After a few months, we moved into a small apartment above a garage at a home in Boylston, Massachusetts. We enjoyed living in the apartment and could walk down the end of the street to the reservoir. There was a small general store across the street that offered excellent pizza and sandwiches.

Our band, *Slant 6 and the Jumpstarts,* played live a few times a month. It was while living in the apartment in Boylston, Massachusetts, that we were performing at the Blue Parrott on Main Street in Worcester. As previously mentioned, on one occasion when we performed, it was the Wednesday before Thanksgiving in 1988. We had an amazing crowd and were asked to give out frozen turkeys to raffle winners between songs.

While living in Boylston, I taught adult literacy at the Opportunities Industrial Center on Main Street in Worcester, while Mary continued working as a nurse. In 1989, I began teaching at the Lighthouse School in Chelmsford, Massachusetts. I was a special education teacher working with students who had severe behavioral issues.

After a few years in the apartment, we bought our first home in a new development on Hickory Lane in Whitinsville, Massachusetts. We had the home built based on our specifications on a lot at the end of the street. We were among the first houses in the development, so it was somewhat dark and isolated.

Mary suggested we get a dog, so we looked for a German Shepherd. She picked out a German Shepherd puppy that she felt a special connection with. We named her Shelby. She was a fantastic dog. When I came home from teaching school, Shelby would bring me one of my running shoes as a reminder that it was time to take her out running. She taught me that pets are equal family members.

We made some wonderful friends and great memories while living on Hickory Lane. Tony and Laurie and their daughter lived close to our house. We would get together for special events, cookouts, going out to dinner and watching the New England Patriots' games.

After four wonderful years living on Hickory Lane, Mary's sister Moira and boyfriend Steve announced they were selling their house at 69 North Street in Grafton, Massachusetts. Mary and I discussed the possibility of buying a home on North Street if we ever moved back to Grafton. It was an easy and direct purchase. Soon after moving in, we put on an addition and expanded the living area.

I had an amazing recording studio built in the basement. This was the new practice and recording area for our band *Slant 6 and the Jumpstarts*. We wrote and recorded many great songs in the studio. Shelby frequently came down and crawled under the recording console where it was quiet and soon earned the nickname "Studio Dog." Our second dog, Emma, enjoyed hanging out with us, finding a quiet place under the console, as well. Emma was a great dog.

Mary began a new career working as a sales representative for Medtronic Corporation. I received and accepted an offer to teach social studies at Grafton Middle School. It was nice being able to walk across the street to work. I enjoyed teaching US history during the first few years as a social studies teacher. It was fascinating to me to make interesting connections between the US history curriculum and the historic people and events in the Grafton and New England area.

When the school shifted from American history to world history, I was disappointed. Every few weeks, I would teach the history of Grafton. I found that most students seemed to enjoy learning about the history of Grafton. I worked with many outstanding teachers during my twenty-four years in the Grafton Public Schools. Deb Kuras was a fantastic teacher's aide who went far beyond the call of duty, providing assistance to not only the special education students but also all the students in my classes.

In late 1999, Mary and I decided to adopt a child. We became involved with Wide Horizons Adoption Agency and took adoption informational classes at the Shrewsbury Public Library. The day we were scheduled to drive down to the Wide Horizon Office in Rhode Island to look through adoption profiles, we received a call from the Wide Horizons Philippines Representative, who had just returned to America. She told us she had found our new daughter, and that there was no need to search through profiles. I have no doubt God strategically planned this. After nine months of processing, we were on a plane to the Philippines to pick up our daughter, Sarah. Upon returning from the Philippines, we took Sarah on vacation to Cape Cod and prepared her to enter the first grade at Grafton Elementary School.

Mark & Sarah – 1st Christmas

Mark & Mary First Christmas with Sarah

Sarah was an excellent student and athlete while attending the Grafton Public Schools. Soccer was her primary sport, while she also enjoyed gymnastics, dance school, track/field, and basketball. She attended a variety of summer camps and loved spending time with her friends. Sarah was an excellent mentor and role model to younger students while in high school.

It was during Sarah's senior year when Mary and I decided to take our lives in a "new direction." While the situation was heartbreaking, that new direction led both of us to amazing places. Ironically, after the divorce proceedings at the Worcester Courthouse, Mary and I went out to lunch together at the Sole Proprietor and had a great time.

Mark, Mary, Sarah - Hobart & William Smith Colleges

Sarah College Graduation

After Sarah graduated from Grafton High School in May 2013, she attended Hobart and William Smith Colleges in Geneva, New York. She played on the soccer team when they won the Division III National Championship in the fall of 2014. We enjoyed attending her soccer games and the many activities in the Finger Lakes area during the four years Sarah attended Hobart and William Smith Colleges.

Our band, *Slant 6 and the Jumpstarts,* was performing live at the Anchor Lounge in Millbury, Massachusetts, on June 16, 2013. During a break, I noticed and recognized Carol, Annie, and Johnny Leofanti, the children of Cathy Harrington, in the audience. Cathy Harrington was the person who trained my brother John to be a dispatcher at the Grafton Police Station. I approached them and asked how their mother Cathy was doing and shared some memories of their grandparents. I felt a powerful connection with Carol and offered her my contact information.

Carol was hesitant to accept my request to contact her. I was able to convince her to let me copy her phone number onto a napkin before returning to the stage to finish our show. After a few days, I called Carol, and the first thing she said to me was that she was not a conversational person and had little or nothing to talk about. We talked nonstop for hours and, to this day, continue to enjoy conversations with each other.

Carol lived in Maine when we first started dating, so I would drive up to see her on weekends. While I continued to live at the house on North Street, I eventually made our summer home in South Yarmouth, Cape Cod, my primary residence. It was a few years before I could retire, so I rented an apartment in Upton, Massachusetts, to stay at during the week to be close to school. I spent my weekends and school vacations at the Cape.

In 2015, I rented an apartment on Worcester Street in Grafton. This allowed for an easy commute to school and the opportunity to be close to Dad, who continued to live at Virginia Circle until he passed in May 2015. I was so glad that Carol was able to get to know Dad, even though it was a short time.

I invited Carol to stay at the house on the Cape, knowing that I would live at the house full time after retirement. Carol accepted a job with Bayada Home Health and worked in the Cape Cod territory.

Carol – Rock & Roll Hall of Fame

Carol and I took a trip across the country during the summer of 2015. Our plan was to drive until we reached an interesting location, only making hotel reservations at the last minute when we were ready to stop. If we liked a certain location, we stayed for a few days.

During the first leg of the trip, we drove to Cleveland, Ohio, and visited the Rock and Roll Hall of Fame. We were impressed, and we recommend everyone visit the museum during their lifetime. Inspired by the show *Man v. Food*, we had lunch at Melt Bar & Grill and enjoyed the most amazing gourmet grilled cheese sandwiches. The next day we went to Avon Lake to see many of the familiar sites I had experienced as a child. After departing Avon Lake, we headed to Michigan and visited the Henry Ford Museum and Greenfield Village. We sat out in front of our hotel on a blanket on the evening of the 4th of July and watched the thousands of fireflies glowing in the night followed by a spectacular fireworks display.

After departing Michigan, we drove across northern Indiana, through Illinois, to Sioux City, Iowa. Cornfields stretched for hundreds of miles along the route. We stayed at the Hard Rock Café Hotel in Sioux City and discovered there was not a Hard Rock Restaurant on site. This made no sense to us because the Hard Rock Café Bar and Restaurant is what identifies the franchise.

Carol - Corn Palace
Mitchell, South Dakota

On our way to South Dakota, we must have seen hundreds of signs advertising Wall Drug. We stopped at a gas station on the way that offered a roadside attraction. If a visitor was willing to pay $1.00, the owner would walk them to the back of the store and open a curtain displaying a stuffed rabbit with deer antlers.

After arriving at Wall Drug, the largest drugstore in the world, we visited Corn Palace. The original Corn Palace was built in the late 1800s to promote the agricultural success of South Dakota. Learning its history fascinated me.

We eventually arrived in the Badlands of South Dakota and stayed at a bed-and-breakfast ranch high on top of a plateau with the most amazing view. We asked if there were any restaurants in the area where we could drive and have dinner. The owners laughed and told us there was a small saloon up the road that served the best "box" frozen pizza in a fifty-mile radius. We enjoyed the cold draft beer and frozen box pizza after it was cooked in the old oven.

Mark – Mt Rushmore 2015

Mount Rushmore was spectacular. We spent a few nights in Deadwood, South Dakota. While in Deadwood, Carol and I visited the Midnight Star Casino, which was owned by actor Kevin Costner at the time. Later in the day, we had drinks at the historic Saloon #10, where James "Wild Bill" Hickok was shot. The blood-stained chair he sat in when he was shot is on display at the saloon. Early the next day, I went for a run up to the top of Boot Hill, where the historic Boot Hill Cemetery is located. Many famous and infamous Wild West personalities are buried there. The hill was so steep, I had to walk as I neared the top to avoid losing my balance.

Devils Tower, Wyoming

After stopping in Sturgis for lunch, we drove to Devils Tower, Wyoming. We stayed at a campground in a rustic cabin for a few nights and were able to watch *Close Encounters of the Third Kind* presented on an outdoor screen every evening at 6:00 p.m. They positioned the screen so you could see Devil's Tower in the distance while watching the movie.

One of the most fascinating museums I have ever visited was the old historic Wyoming State Prison. We were able to see the jail cell where Butch Cassidy was imprisoned for a short time and one of the earliest gas chambers ever installed at a prison.

Next, we headed southward to Zion National Park and Park City, Utah. Inside Zion National Park was a small "ghost" town called Grafton. It was a long ride on a rustic dirt road to get there. I am glad we had a Jeep.

Our next stop was Las Vegas, Nevada. We stayed at the Bellagio Resort & Casino and went to see the show *O* by Cirque du Soleil. The following day, we visited the Atomic Test Site Museum and Hoover Dam. It was 124 degrees at Hoover Dam, but I did not mind the dry heat. Carol was uncomfortable, so we limited our time outside. I preferred the extreme dry heat over temperatures with high humidity and dew points.

We took a train ride to the Grand Canyon and saw elk grazing in the surrounding hills. The canyon was spectacular, and during the return trip, our train was "robbed" by cowboys. They came on board the train and walked around with hats, asking if anyone would like to donate to a charity.

We departed the Grand Canyon and drove to Flagstaff, Arizona, and stayed at the historic Monte Vista Hotel on Route 66. The only room available was the presidential suite for $116.00 per night. I asked why every room in the hotel was booked but the suite. They told us it was haunted. The presidential suite was red, with gold and black trim. After settling in, I was in the bathroom shaving and I kept hearing a woman's voice saying, "Hello!"

I eventually opened the bathroom door and asked Carol why she was saying hello to me so loudly. Carol told me it was not her. All night, Carol and I heard music from somewhere in or around the building. The next morning at checkout, we informed the desk clerk about our experiences and were told that there were no bands playing in the area and many people had had similar experiences staying in that suite.

Our next stop was Old Albuquerque, New Mexico. We stayed in a Mexican-style villa and enjoyed authentic Mexican food. There were skunks running around the center garden area, and Carol was afraid of being sprayed. Fortunately, the skunks didn't spray us.

**Mark 2015
Cross Country Trip**

As we traveled east on historic Route 66, we pulled over to see the many closed-down roadside hotels, shops, and restaurants. It was sad to see so many vacant buildings and ghost towns. Route 66 is an amazing piece of American history that is slowly disappearing.

Fortunately, Carol noticed we had driven past the roadside attraction referred to as Cadillac Ranch. We did a quick U-turn and walked up a short dirt road to see the half-buried Cadillac automobiles sticking out of the ground.

While driving through Northern Texas, our windshield was covered with splattered locusts that plagued the area. We stopped and had dinner at The Big Texas Steakhouse that we had seen featured on *Man v. Food*. We did not attempt to do the 72-ounce steak challenge but observed a man who had agreed to try. If a person can eat a 72-ounce steak along with the sides in an hour or less, it is free. If a person fails the challenge, they must pay $100.00 for the meal. We left before he completed the challenge but learned that few people ever succeeded.

Driving through the Smoky Mountains in Tennessee was spectacular. We stayed at a few places along the way and enjoyed the scenery. One of our last stops before returning home was Hershey, Pennsylvania. We had been there a few times and stayed at Hershey Lodge. We visited Hershey World and explored Main Street in the downtown area. I stocked up on Hershey chocolate and bought some Hershey T-shirts while there.

Our last stop was at the historic Hotel Fauchère in the Pocono Mountains. We spent a relaxing night at the hotel and departed early the next morning. Traveling across and around the country with Carol was my adventure of a lifetime. I am blessed and thankful to have been able to take such a trip. We hope to do it again soon.

After Dad passed, I moved back to Virginia Circle during the weekdays until my retirement in June 2017. As previously mentioned, I was able to convince Carol to live at the house in South Yarmouth while I finished my last few years teaching at Grafton Middle School. Carol worked for Bayada Home Health Care out of the Cape Cod office. I would go to the Cape House on weekends.

After retiring from the Grafton Public Schools, Carol and I bought a beautiful stone home in the Historic Stone Village in Chester, Vermont, that was for sale. After completing some renovations to the house, we opened the Stone House Bed and Breakfast in the fall of 2018. We also created a kettle corn company, using the small stone building next to the house as a place to manufacture the kettle corn. We enjoyed operating the bed and breakfast and kettle corn company and were able to meet some interesting people who either stayed with us or came to the shop to purchase kettle corn. When in the mood, I would set up a table and sell kettle corn at some of the local farmer's markets.

The stone house had an apartment above the garage, and in 2019, we took in two special-needs adults who needed to learn how to live independently. While COVID-19 created some new challenges with the business and mentoring the two special needs adults, we did well.

Stone House Bed & Breakfast

Garden Photo

While living in the stone house, there was a ghost or spirit of a woman that spoke to us on multiple occasions. She would say, "Hello," or "Who are you?" She had a clear, distinct voice and seemed relaxed and friendly. There was one occasion, while standing in the kitchen, when Carol and I were talking to one of the young ladies we mentored and, right next to us, we heard her say, "Hello." The three of us looked at each other and confirmed with each other what we had just heard.

One day while taking pictures of some flowers in her garden, Carol was able to capture a picture of this woman "materializing" on a single-frame digital photo. "Ghost Hunters," who would stay with us at the bed-and-breakfast, informed us that the photo was amazing and how difficult it was to capture a photo of a materializing spirit. It is rare to capture movement in a single digital-frame photo.

I experienced multiple incidents when alone in the house or in the cooper house when she would say hello. Whenever this happened, I responded by saying hello and then told her to go towards and enter "the light." I am confident she eventually followed my advice.

One day while cleaning my kettle corn equipment, she said hello. I told her she would find friends and loved ones in the bright light. Immediately after saying this, the cooper house door flew open and then slammed shut again. I went outside to see if someone had opened and shut the door from the outside, but there was nobody there. We never heard from her again.

Head Case Creations LLC Tradeshow

In 2020, Carol's brother Johnny created a prototype of a new device he invented that protects fire sprinkler heads during construction. Carol offered Johnny her marketing and organizational skills while I became involved with filing provisional patents, a utility patent, and a trademark. My good friend Ken Holland, a semi-retired engineer, provided professional CAD drawings while making detailed modifications and improvements to the devices. Johnny, Ken, Carol and I soon became owners of our new company, Head Case Creations, LLC. We currently have these devices being manufactured at Ash Industries in Lafayette, Louisiana, and available for purchase through Colony Hardware out of Orange, Connecticut.

After five years of running a successful business, Carol and I sold the home in Vermont and started a new chapter together. We currently enjoy living on the coast of Maine for eight months during the spring, summer, and fall, and spending the winter months in Florida visiting Carol's sister, Andrea, husband, Steve, and their amazing son, Jake. I continue to work with our band, *Slant 6 and the Jumpstarts,* while helping oversee the business side of Head Case Creations LLC. I am still addicted to lifting weights, running, and biking. Most importantly, I continue to enjoy my time and life with Carol and daughter, Sarah. I am so fortunate and blessed to have Carol and Sarah in my life.

**Mark & Carol – Sunset at the Beach
Clearwater, Florida**

Mark & Carol   **Mark & Sarah**

CHAPTER 23

Paul Joseph Ouellette

Paul was the fourth of seven children and quite gifted with athletic speed and agility. Throughout elementary and middle school, Paul won trophies and occasionally broke school records while participating in the Presidential Physical Fitness Program. Over time, he developed his musical skills and became an amazing guitar player. Paul's work ethic and commitment to any job he did after graduation from high school never ceased to amaze me.

Paul was born at Fairview Park Hospital in Cleveland, Ohio, on November 18, 1959, and baptized a few weeks later. Back then, new mothers and their babies were required to stay in the hospital for two or three days before being released. I remember Dad taking John Jr., James, and me to the hospital parking lot every evening while Mom was in the hospital so we could look up and wave while she held Paul up to the window. Because of health and patient safety concerns, kids were not permitted to enter the hospital at that time.

It was an exciting moment, and I later realized that I was no longer the youngest child in the family. After about ten or fifteen minutes of smiling and waving, we headed back home so Dad could heat TV dinners for us. It seemed unusual to have Dad do everything Mom usually did when she was home. I sensed the excitement Dad was experiencing with the birth of their fourth child and his ability to adapt and become both a mother and father for a few days.

Having a new younger brother created a new family dynamic. Over time, I realized how good Mom and Dad were at treating us equally, yet still as unique individuals, allowing us to seek our own interests and hobbies.

With the arrival of Paul into our family, it was established that John Jr. and James would share a bedroom while Paul and I shared another while living in Avon Lake, Ohio, Lorton, Virginia, and later Grafton, Massachusetts. While living in Avon Lake, Paul and I used the upstairs hallway as our bedroom. We did not have an actual bedroom to share until we moved to Lorton, Virginia, in 1970.

Lois & Paul at his 1st Communion

I remember Paul being a good student while in elementary school. Eventually, he began taking part in the afternoon and weekend activities Dad planned. One of Paul's favorite activities was swimming at the Avon Lake Public Pool. I clearly remember the day Dad taught Paul how to swim as I watched John and Jim dive off the high-level diving board. Paul could dive off the high diving board soon after learning how to swim.

There was a measuring stick mounted on the side of the diving board ladder. A person had to be a certain height to access the high diving board. Everyone had to wait in line until the lifeguard gave the "OK" signal to climb up the ladder to the diving board. Paul did not hesitate to jump off the high diving board his first time and even put on a good show by twisting and contorting his body while making funny faces. His performance impressed me.

I remember the day Dad took us to the local army surplus store and purchased army bunk beds with single-layer military mattresses. These beds were pretty comfortable, and I thought it was neat to sleep in authentic army bunk beds. I chose the bottom bunk while Paul slept on the top bunk right above me. Every so often, I got in trouble for putting my feet up in the air and pushing on the bottom of his mattress.

It was fun sharing a room with Paul when we were young children, around five and six years old. We would have what we called "Teddy Bear Meetings." The meetings began with each of us selecting a stuffed animal and, like bad ventriloquists, we simulated the stuffed animals talking to each other in high squeaky voices. The interactions during these silly "Teddy Bear Meetings" started out calm and pleasant. Eventually, the interactive conversations escalated to the point of teddy bear "violence," with the stuffed animals hitting and punching each other until our mother shouted up the stairs, "Please go to sleep!"

Paul Ouellette
Grade 3

Being the youngest, Paul suffered most during our TV commercial wrestling matches. Mom described these wrestling matches to me many years later. She told me that on Saturdays and Sundays after breakfast, John, Jim, Paul, and I watched a movie while waiting for Dad to take us out for some kind of afternoon activity. We liked to watch *The Bowery Boys, Tarzan*, and any of the old black and white horror and monster movies.

Paul Ouellette
Grade 5

While the movie was playing, we were quiet and focused, but the moment a commercial break started, it was an all-out wrestling match with yelling, banging and loud thuds until the movie came back on. Paul was the only brother I could come close to pinning down. At times, John and Jim wrestled each other or simply teamed up to conquer

Paul and me. The goal of the wrestling match was to pin down your opponent before the movie resumed. Occasionally, we teamed up against John, usually resulting in an injury because John was bigger and stronger than the rest of us. Paul tried his hardest, but as the youngest, he suffered more injuries.

In the mid-1960s, Paul had a pet alligator. This was an excellent example of how our parents allowed and encouraged us to seek our own hobbies and interests. He also had some pet turtles around the same time.

Paul did not hesitate to seek out his own group of friends. He had no issues speaking with girls in and above his age group. I was impressed with his ability to make friends and hang out with boys and girls his age. I was shy and much more hesitant to talk with girls when in elementary school.

Following Paul's first communion, Dad took him to the Aqua Marine Restaurant for breakfast. Going out for breakfast after a first communion had already become a family tradition. I remember Paul going to communion and making "cross-eyed" facial gestures as he walked back to our pew. He would do this when Mom and Dad were not looking, causing me to laugh. He did this to me for some time, and I eventually learned to shut my eyes as he returned from communion.

Paul Ouellette Early 1970s at train car next to Cumberland Farms in Grafton Center

In my opinion, Paul was the best overall athlete in our family. His ability to win the Presidential Fitness Award year after year was impressive. His speed in the fifty-yard dash, distance achieved in the long jump, and ability to throw the softball were far superior to my athletic skills.

When Paul was a freshman at Grafton High School, I was a sophomore and Jim was a senior. Jim and I convinced Paul to join the Grafton High School track team. On the second day of track practice, Paul was able to run an unofficial 100-yard sprint that tied the state record of 10.1 seconds.

Paul was a talented artist. He painted a picture of our previous home in Lorton, Virginia, from a photograph of the house.

While living in Lorton, Virginia, between December 1970 and April 1972, Paul and I liked to hang out together more often than we did in Avon Lake. We shared a large bedroom and enjoyed watching our thirteen-inch black-and-white TV. We spent many Friday nights together watching Sir Graves Ghastly, who hosted classic horror movies while performing humorous skits during commercial breaks.

While living in Lorton, Paul and I wrote a song while walking to Hanlin's store, about a mile up the road from our house. We both started clicking our fingers and singing, "I got the beat, walking down the street." The song evolved into a ballad about one of our neighbors, Jeff, and his broken minibike. Ironically, it became a song that our band, *Slant 6 and the Jumpstarts,* would perform during practices for many years. We never professionally recorded it or released it on any of our cassettes or CDs. This has been one of my favorite original songs our band did.

Near our home in Lorton, about a mile down a steep hill, is a small village named Occoquan. The town of Occoquan was built along the Occoquan River and is known for its Civil War history and 19th-century fishing industry.

In the early spring, Paul and I rode our bikes down the steep hill and went fishing when the herring were "running." We used a three-pronged hook to cast and snag the fish, no bait required. There were people who scooped up the fish with long-handled fishing nets. We brought home buckets of herring that we filleted, packed in salt and stored in our large freezer.

In the morning, while getting ready for school, we saw a commercial advertising a new toy called the "Footsie." This was a gadget you put around your ankle and spun like a hula-hoop. Paul and I sang the jingle for that commercial over and over, "Footsie, wow, everybody's having fun!" We also liked to whistle the theme song to the *Three Stooges* cartoon that always seemed to be on television while getting ready for school in the morning.

In late 1971, Dad requested a transfer to the FBI Headquarters in Boston. Fortunately, thanks to Dad's loyalty and commitment to the FBI, Hoover granted the transfer. Many years later, Dad told me he was concerned about the communication problems between President Nixon and Hoover and did not want to be one of the "in-between" agents delivering messages back and forth. Dad was happy to be out of Washington in time to avoid the Watergate incident.

Paul Ouellette fishing at Silver Lake in Grafton, MA 1988

Following his graduation from Grafton High School, Paul did not hesitate to work full time. He worked at Corrugated Manufacturing for a time and then at a swimming pool manufacturing company, building pools in Ohio. I remember Paul talking about his experiences building swimming pools and his occasional visits to our former hometown, Avon Lake, Ohio. He earned his CDL license after attending the New England Tractor Trailer School. He worked for a few trucking companies until he landed a job with Certus Inc., currently Dana Transportation Inc.

When they were kids, Dad was friends with Mr. Polselli Sr., who eventually began the Polselli and Sons Construction Firm in North Grafton, Massachusetts. It was nice to know the Polsellis because we had many things in common; we attended the same church, both our families had seven children, and there were friendships between the kids. Paul was driving one of the Polselli's trucks, delivering jet fuel to New York City when 9/11 occurred and was stuck on the George Washington Bridge for many hours.

Paul eventually became a member of the "Million Mile Club," the highest honor a truck driver can earn. This is equivalent to driving to the moon and back twice.

Jim remembers when Paul would contribute to a charity by filling shoeboxes with toys and school supplies. He emphasized that Paul really enjoyed doing this.

Paul Ouellette
Passport Picture Late 1970s

Paul Ouellette – Virginia Circle

Eventually, Paul would get married and have two children.

As previously mentioned, Paul is an amazing guitar player. He was an important part of the formation and advancement of our band, *Slant 6 and the Jumpstarts*. In the mid-1980s, he performed on our first professional recordings at Pine Trax Studio in Holyoke, Massachusetts. He played the lead guitar tracks on our first 45 RPM single titled "Pull the Plug."

Hundreds of radio stations around the nation played this song. Paul played lead guitar on other tracks that appeared on our first cassette album titled *Browns Road*. Paul performed with us at our first live performance at the Shrewsbury Sportsman Club in Shrewsbury, Massachusetts, during the summer of 1986.

Paul has amazing talent and skill working with wood. At one point, Paul was making birdhouses and walking sticks as a side hobby. He made an amazing walking stick that was given to me as a gift. As a joke, I told people it was the original walking stick used by Johnny Appleseed. I had the walking stick on display in my kettle corn shop when Carol and I were running the Stone House Bed and Breakfast and Kettle Corn Company in Chester, Vermont.

As a devoted Grateful Dead and Frank Zappa fan, Paul enjoyed playing their music. I've lost count of how many times I've been at a party where he pulled out his acoustic guitar and played for the crowd, creating an upbeat sing-along.

Paul is an excellent cook. His chili, tacos, cornbread, homemade pizza, and grilled cheese sandwiches are classic. It is amazing what can be learned from each other when growing up in a large family. Paul taught me that life should be fun and never to be afraid to take a chance.

CHAPTER 24

Marie Elizabeth Ouellette

After giving birth to four boys, our mother was excited to finally welcome a baby girl into the family. I remember Dad taking John, Jim, Paul, and me to Lakewood Hospital the day after Marie was born so we could wave to Mom from the parking lot while she held up baby Marie in front of her hospital bedroom window. I remember Dad telling us we now had a sister and needed to be gentle when playing with her.

Marie Elizabeth Ouellette was born on Saturday, July 28, 1962, at 5:57 p.m. at Lakewood Hospital in Lakewood, Ohio. She was baptized a couple of weeks later. Mom and Dad were so happy to have a daughter. Marie brought a new dynamic to our family. I could see how much Mom enjoyed engaging in mother-daughter activities. There were now dolls and other girl-related gifts appearing under our Christmas trees and on her birthdays. She never had to worry about her brothers taking any of her toys.

Marie Ouellette

Marie was an excellent student in elementary school, middle school, high school, and college. In my opinion, Marie was the most dedicated and academically gifted child in our family. She seemed to enjoy doing homework and participating in school activities.

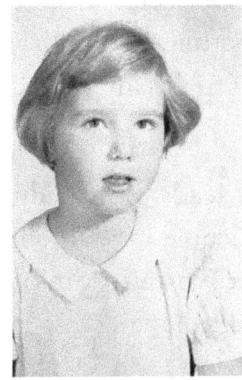

**Marie Ouellette
Kindergarten**

While Marie was in the second grade at Westview Elementary School in Avon Lake, there was a bomb scare. Dad, along with other FBI agents, came into the school and searched for bombs. He took the time to say hello to Marie and told her she had nothing to worry about.

Mom and Dad were very protective of Marie. We learned quickly not to tease her. I have the highest respect for Marie and how she was able to cope with four older brothers and eventually, two younger brothers. It would be fascinating to read a book about growing up in an FBI family as the only girl out of seven children, from her perspective.

When I was a senior at Grafton High School, Marie was a freshman. I became protective of Marie and, for the first time, started to really get to know her. I asked my fellow senior friends to say hello to her in the hallways when they saw her.

Marie Ouellette

Marie played tennis while attending Grafton High School. She did well in her classes and was gifted in mathematics. Her math teacher inspired her to major in mathematics after graduating from Grafton High School.

Following her graduation from Grafton High School in May 1980, Marie attended Quinsigamond Community College in Worcester, Massachusetts. She earned an Associate of Science degree in Business Data Processing in the spring of 1982. While attending classes at Quinsigamond

Community College, she held a part-time job working for New England Power in Westboro, Massachusetts, as a junior clerk in the Revenue Accounting Department. Marie worked at Caldor's Department Store in Westboro, Massachusetts, in the Retail Sales Department. Caldor's, a discount department store chain, was founded in 1951. Many looked upon it as being the "Bloomingdale's of discounting."

In the late 1970s or early 1980s, Marie became good friends with Sandy, who lived with her family on North Street in Grafton Center. In addition, she was good friends with Sue Chartier, who lived on Worcester Street, and Laura Holland, who was a few years younger and lived on Virginia Circle.

Marie has an amazing voice, plays the guitar, and is an excellent piano player. Whenever I heard Marie playing piano in the basement, I would go down to the basement and play along on guitar or keep a steady beat on Neal's drum set. My fondest memories of jamming together in the basement were around Thanksgiving and Christmas. Marie and I enjoyed playing traditional Christmas music.

In 1979, we began to play together in the basement as a rock band. Marie played the piano, Neal was on drums, Paul played guitar, Jim performed vocals, and I played bass guitar. Soon after, we began calling ourselves *Slant 6 and the Jumpstarts.* John became involved by recording many of these "jam" sessions on his Radio Shack Realistic two-track recorder and videotaping some sessions on his VHS equipment. Marie provided amazing vocals for our first professional recordings at Pine Trax Studio in Holyoke, Massachusetts, in the early to mid-1980s.

In 1982, Marie worked in the retail department at Spags Discount Store in Shrewsbury, Massachusetts. Spags Discount Store has an amazing history. Anthony Borgatti Jr., better known as Spags, graduated from high school in 1934 and opened an automotive hardware store in a section of a building his parents owned on Route 9 in Shrewsbury,

Massachusetts. Over time, he offered a variety of products that were requested by customers. His down-to-earth friendliness made him one of the most popular and respected businessmen in all of Worcester County.

Marie loves making puzzles. The screened porch on the side of our house in Grafton became a place where she and Mom could sit for hours at a time working on puzzles. These puzzles consisted of thousands of pieces and could be pretty challenging. Occasionally, Marie would glue a completed puzzle to a sheet of cardboard, place it in a frame, and hang it on a wall in the basement. Everyone enjoyed looking at these puzzle exhibits. I was impressed by the skills and patience Marie and Mom showed in completing such masterpieces.

Marie attended Boston College in the 1980s and owned a car with the letters "BC" painted on both sides. I thought that was cool.

I remember Marie having a small party at our house and inviting some of her Boston College friends. They were all nice people, and I enjoyed meeting students from what I considered to be a prestigious school.

Marie worked at Wyman Gordon in North Grafton for a period in the 1980s. Wyman Gordon, formally known as Air Force Plant 63, was built by the United States Airforce in 1946 and purchased by Wyman Gordon in 1982. The plant is home to one of our nation's largest forging presses. Marie was a member of the Wyman Gordon Credit Union and enjoyed the benefits the credit union offered.

While in college, it was much cheaper to go out to the railroad tracks behind our house to make a bonfire and hang out than it was to go to clubs and bars, which I didn't particularly enjoy—especially disco clubs. Because of my enrollment as a postgraduate at Worcester Academy in 1978, and taking a year off from college in 1979, I did not start my full-time college career until 1980, the year Marie graduated from Grafton High School.

Marie and I were in similar financial situations, being enrolled in college full time while working part time. Marie and I thought these "Railroad Track Parties" were the perfect opportunity to have fun, not drive anywhere and save money. These gatherings started out small and soon escalated to anywhere from a few people to perhaps fifteen or twenty people. There were always surprise guests, and we never knew who might show up. Eventually, Neal and Rich and some of their friends attended these Friday night bonfires.

L - R Sue Chartier, Marie Ouellette,
Elisa Ouellette, Mark Ouellette
Elisa Baptism

Marie & Elisa
Dayton, TN 1987

Marie gave birth to her first child, Elisa, on September 16, 1982. This was a blessing and brought new opportunities for the entire family. I was so excited to be an uncle. Mom and Dad were excited to be grandparents. Elisa had six uncles who enjoyed the youthful energy and excitement she brought to the family.

Marie eventually went to England to teach at a private school. She spent a significant amount of time living and working in England. While in England, she met James Towersey. They eventually married and had a wonderful daughter named Becky. Marie, along with her husband James, would occasionally come back to Grafton to visit during the summer. Marie would set up a small TV on a table under the tree in the front yard at Virginia Circle and watch tennis matches. Occasionally, they would come back and visit during the holidays.

Becky Towersey

In the late 1980s, when Mary and I were living in a small apartment in Boylston, Massachusetts, Marie came over on a Saturday afternoon to go fishing with me at the reservoir located a short walk down the street. She brought her guitar, and while fishing, we wrote a song called "Mrs. Fletcher, Help Me, I've Fallen." This song eventually became a huge hit for our band, *Slant 6 and the Jumpstarts,* topping radio station charts around the country and other parts of the world.

Eventually, Marie moved back to the United States and continued teaching and enjoying her hobbies and musical interests. Marie played an important role in my life and helped me to learn and understand how important it is to unconditionally support and protect immediate family. I have many amazing memories growing up in a family of six boys and one girl.

CHAPTER 25

Neal Matthew Ouellette

At fourteen, I recall standing in our Grafton kitchen as Mom cooked fried pinto bean pancakes. Neal and Rich were sitting at the dining room table playing a board game. As I watched Mom cook, I heard Neal and Rich arguing about the rules of the game. I looked at Mom and asked, "Which of the seven children in our family was the easiest baby to deal with?" She quickly replied, "Neal."

L – R Rich & Neal
Mid 1970s

Neal was born on August 29, 1965, at Lakewood Hospital in Lakewood, Ohio, and was baptized at St. Joseph Church a few weeks later. I was seven years old, and I remember how excited Mom was when returning home from the hospital with "baby" Neal. As I mentioned, Neal was the easiest and most cooperative baby out of the seven children, but Mom said Marie came in at a close second.

On Thanksgiving morning in 1969, when Neal was around four years old, Mom allowed him to come outside and play touch football with us. Before we went in for Thanksgiving dinner, Dad told us to let Neal score a touchdown. We had so much fun running up to him and purposely falling to the ground as though he were knocking us over.

As with all of us, Mom was protective when we were young, but she let me take Neal for short hikes down to the apple orchard and creek occasionally. I would bring my Daisy BB gun and allow Neal to shoot at cans with me.

Neal liked to hang out with us when we made campfires in our fire pit. I remember teaching Neal how to cook marshmallows using a long stick we would cut down in the old wheat field behind our house. I would take Neal with me to pick apples for Mom when she wanted to make applesauce.

There was a large family room in our home in Avon Lake where we could play with toys and board games, watch TV, listen to the radio, read comics, or relax on rainy days. This was where Mom kept her piano and a table for making puzzles. Neal enjoyed playing Operation, Mouse Trap and building log cabins with Lincoln Logs.

While living in Lorton, Virginia, during the early 1970s, I continued to take Neal with me on short hikes and to check my wooden box traps I built out of scrap wood. There was a path behind our house that went to a small pond across the street from the Alcoholic Rehabilitation Center.

One day, Neal and I were hiking to the pond, and we came upon a large black water moccasin snake. I stopped and used my right hand to guide and position Neal behind me to protect him from the snake. Holding my BB gun in my left hand, I took out my hunting knife and threw it at the snake, cutting half of its head off instantly. I had spent a lot of time practicing knife-throwing skills with little or no success. I was incredibly lucky that day.

After moving to Grafton, I remember Dad taking Neal, Marie, and Rich to the movies. I had become old enough to go to the movie theater on my own, but enjoyed hearing Marie, Neal, and Rich talk about the movies they had seen. There was a lot of excitement after seeing *Willy Wonka and the Chocolate Factory, Bedknobs and Broomsticks, The Aristocats, The Bad News Bears, Benji* and *Herbie* movies, to name a few. Neal and Rich were at the right age to enjoy the television debuts of *A Year Without Santa Claus* 1974, *Rudolph's Shiny New Year* 1976 and *The Little Drummer Boy* 1976.

Moving to Grafton allowed Neal and Rich the opportunity to enjoy their early childhood in a safe neighborhood. Neal and Rich had become good friends with Tom and Paul Holland, who lived on our street. They played together and participated in local organized sports. I remember seeing Neal and Rich riding their bikes around town and wondering where they were going?

Neal and some of his friends built an amazing one-room cabin in the woods behind our house. I was excited when Neal asked me if I wanted to see the cabin he and his friends built. The cabin was amazing. It had a wood stove, chairs to sit in, and was close to our house.

When Neal was in elementary school, he loved to eat Dinty Moore canned beef stew. It was quick and easy to make. As a result, we called him "Dinty."

Neal played baseball in the Grafton Farm League. He was an excellent pitcher. When time allowed, I went to see him play at the Norcross Baseball Field on North Street. Dad was at many of these games, and it was fun to sit with him and watch Neal play.

Neal Kindgergarten
Lorton, VA

On one occasion, I drove my 1974 AMC Gremlin to one of his games at the Norcross baseball field. I sat with Dad at the game, and after a few innings, a Grafton police officer walked up to us and asked me to move my car from the front lawn of the house across the street from the park. Embarrassed, I crossed the street and moved my car back to the parking lot.

After conducting research, I discovered that AMC Gremlins were known to pop out of park and go into neutral if on a hill or decline. My emergency brake did not work, which explained the situation. It was after this incident that I kept a couple of bricks in my car to wedge under the wheels when parking on a hill or slight decline.

Neal played football while attending Grafton High School. During this time, I would take him with me to work out at City Health Club. He played offensive guard and then, as a senior, became a captain of the team. He switched positions and played fullback his senior year.

Neal played on the St. Philip's Catholic Youth Conference basketball team while in high school. He was a strong rebounder and an excellent defensive player. I was coach, and our team won the Catholic Youth Conference Basketball Championship his senior year.

My players had some fun parties, and it was nice to see them play and hang out together. I was invited to one of these basketball parties and felt a little awkward because of my age and position.

**Neal's Confirmation
St. Philips 1980s**

There were also some cheerleaders from another town, whom they had met and invited to the party. I was about seven years older than the members on my team but had a great time.

Neal is an excellent drummer and has been involved with our band, *Slant 6 and the Jumpstarts,* since 1979. He was fourteen and available to play drums when we "jammed" on Saturday mornings. The original band consisted of Jim on vocals, Marie playing piano, Paul on guitar, and me playing bass guitar. John recorded our performances on a two-track tape machine and occasionally videotaped these early sessions.

Eventually, Neal introduced his friend Gary Dussault to the band. Gary played the guitar in our band for many years. When Paul went on the road as a long-distance truck driver, Gary introduced guitarist Don Thurber to the band. The band's philosophy was that anyone who wanted to come to practices and participate in our jam session was welcome. Eventually, the core of the band included Jim Ouellette, Neal Ouellette, Mark Ouellette, Gary Dussault, and Don Thurber. Occasionally, Mike Sheehan, "Bongo Mike," came to practice to play bongos and perform with us at some of our live shows.

Marie and Paul contributed to many of our recording sessions when available. Rich was our roadie, helping us load and unload equipment at live performance locations. Ken Holland videotaped many of our live shows and recording sessions. My friend Rich helped us create an excellent promotional video in the late 1980s.

Neal Ouellette Early 1980s

It was the mid-1980s when Neal and I were in my 1974 Dodge Dart traveling down Grafton Street toward Kelly Square in Worcester. Suddenly, we heard a bang, and the car went totally dead. Luckily, momentum kept us rolling down the hill while I looked in my rearview mirror and saw the entire transmission of the car sitting in the middle of the road. As we rolled toward Kelly Square, every traffic light was green, and we eventually made it to the gas station on the opposite side of the square. I was lucky that I never needed to use my brakes to slow down or stop the car.

The manager came out and told us we could not leave the car there. I told him I would have the car towed at some point. I was attending graduate school and could not afford to deal with the time and expense of towing a car, knowing it was useless. We walked up the street to a phone booth and called home for a ride. John ended up coming to our rescue and brought us back to Virginia Circle. I never saw that car again.

Neal worked at Mayflower Moving Company during the mid to late 1980s. This was a perfect job for college students or anyone who was willing to work hard to make good money. Neal, Rich and I worked many jobs together. Jim worked at Mayflower when he had free time or was transitioning between jobs.

I remember how excited Neal was when he received the Pink Floyd album *The Wall* in 1979. He played that record repeatedly for some time. Neal loved the album so much that he bought additional copies and hung one on his wall as a decoration. He used the others to replace the ones he had worn out from overplaying.

Following his graduation from Grafton High School, Neal continued to maintain friendships with Paul Holland, Tom Holland, Jamey, and the McDonough boys, Mark, Joe, and John.

Neal formally introduced me to Mr. and Mrs. McDonough when I was invited to join their Fantasy Football group. You could count on the McDonough boys to be at our live performances and at Norcross field on Worcester Street Thanksgiving mornings to play touch football.

Neal attended Worcester State College and received a Bachelor of Arts in Psychology in May 1990. He then attended Fitchburg State University, where he earned a Master of Education in Moderate Special Needs in May 2003.

Neal worked as a crisis intervention counselor at Lighthouse School in Chelmsford, Massachusetts, from August 1990 to 1998. He counseled a diverse population of students with emotional, intellectual, health, autism, and physical disabilities ranging in age from three to twenty-two. Ironically, this was where I taught special education from 1989 to 1993 before taking a full-time social studies position at Grafton Middle School.

Neal & Marie Wedding

Neal and I worked together at Lighthouse School for about three years. We made a few good friends at school and had a great time working together. It was at Lighthouse School that Neal met his future wife, Marie. Neal and Marie were married on June 29, 2002, at St. Francis Church in Dracut, Massachusetts. I believe it was at their wedding when I first met Marie's wonderful mother, Cecille, for the first time. The wedding was awesome, and the reception was fun.

Neal and Marie eventually bought a home in the Worcester County area. They have a son, John, and a daughter, Julia, both intelligent, polite, and musically talented. John plays the saxophone (baritone, tenor, alto, and soprano), clarinet (clarinet, bass clarinet, and contrabass clarinet) trombone, flute, and piano. Julia plays the trombone and the flute. She enjoys working with and riding horses.

Dad enjoyed seeing John and Julia at their birthday parties and holiday celebrations Neal and his wife Marie hosted at their home. Neal would bring the kids to Virginia Circle to play the "rock toss" game with Dad. They would draw a target with chalk on the edge of the street and see who could toss a pebble closest to the center. The game was fun and a chance for Dad to bond with his grandchildren. After working at Lighthouse School, Neal served as a special education teacher working with students with severe intellectual and physical disabilities in grades four through seven.

In August 2000, Neal accepted a position as a special education teacher at a public school in Southern Worcester County. Neal continues to teach special education and plans to retire soon.

L - R John & Julia Ouellette

As of the writing of this chapter, Neal and Marie continue to enjoy family life while John and Julia attend college. As previously mentioned, John and Julia are blessed and gifted with remarkable musical talents. I know some of these talents were genetically passed down from our mother. I am confident that Mom and Dad are extremely proud of what Neal has accomplished so far in life.

CHAPTER 26

Richard Lawrence Ouellette

Richard was the seventh and final child our parents brought into the world. He was born on September 17, 1968, at Lakewood Hospital in Lakewood, Ohio. Father Kenneth J. Wolnowski baptized Richard at St. Joseph Parish on September 29th, 1968.

Lois & Rich
Early 1970s Lorton, VA

I was nine years old when Rich was born and remember how energetic he was as a baby. Jim remembers Mom coming home with Rich and Dad taking the door off a large closet in the hallway outside of their bedroom and placing a crib inside. The hallway was where Paul and I slept on bunk beds. Mom and Dad kept their bedroom door open while Rich was in his crib. I remember only a few occasions when Rich was crying, and Mom would come out to attend to him.

Soon after learning how to walk, Mom allowed Rich to run around the house as much as possible while putting up gates to keep him in designated areas. After Rich learned to walk, Mom occasionally let me take him outside to play catch or have him run sprints holding a small football. On a few occasions, Jim brought "baby" Richard with him to ride around on the backhoes that were parked behind our house in Avon Lake. This was where a new apartment complex was being built. The workers often left the keys inside the construction equipment over the weekend, and Jim would sneak over and drive the backhoes around the field behind our house. Jim, who was only eleven or twelve years old, would put "baby" Rich on his lap and take him for rides around the construction area. As a child, Rich loved grape Kool-Aid and could never get enough of it. Jim and I used to call him "purple teeth kid."

While living in Lorton, Virginia, between December 1970 and April 1972, Richard was three and four years old. He would go outside and walk over to Mr. and Mrs. Carlsons' house, our neighbors next door, to watch the birds drink water from their bird bath. Seeing little Richard, Mrs. Carlson would head outside, hoping to give him a hug. The moment Rich saw her walking toward him, he would run back home to avoid inter-action. I would have done the same thing.

Richard Grafton, MA
Mid 1970s

Rich Elementary School

Rich attended the Grafton Public Schools from kindergarten in 1973 through his graduation from Grafton High School in May 1986. He was the only Ouellette child to experience most of his public school education in the same school system. He spent only a few months at the American Elementary School when Mom and Dad were in Saudi Arabia.

Moving to Grafton and living on Virginia Circle was an excellent opportunity for Rich to enjoy growing up in a small town where there was little crime and plenty of kids to play with. In my opinion, Rich and Neal had a special bond because of how close they were in age. They had many friends in the neighborhood and in the town of Grafton.

Rich celebrated his first penance at Saint Philip's Parish in Grafton on November 18, 1975, while in the fourth grade. Father Raymond Lounge performed the ceremony. Father Lounge was a priest one might describe as the deliverer of "fire and brimstone" homilies.

Father Lounge orchestrated the construction of the new parish building in the late 1970s, which included an enclosed soundproof room with a large glass window overlooking the pews and the altar. This was where families with young children were expected to take part in Mass. Prior to the construction of the new church and what we called the "crybaby" room, Father Lounge would stop speaking during Mass if a small baby began crying. He would sit and stare at the parents of the child until the child stopped crying, or the parents took the infant outside.

L - R Rich & Mark Ouellette
Cape Cod Mid 1970s

Rich received the sacrament of confirmation on April 16, 1984. Bishop Timothy J. Harris was present, along with our new pastor, Reverend Richard E. Collette. Richard attended CCD classes that were offered at our church, St. Philip's.

When I graduated from high school in May 1977, Rich was in the fourth grade. I was busy preparing to attend Worcester Academy as a postgraduate student. I remember coming home after school and watching *The Gong Show* with Rich before doing my homework. We both laughed and enjoyed watching "Gene, Gene the Dancing Machine" when he would make a special appearance.

I recall watching the horror movie *Phantasm* with Rich one Friday night in the early 1980s. Rich was in eighth or ninth grade, and we were scared.

After Paul moved out, Rich and I shared my original bedroom at Virginia Circle while I attended undergraduate and graduate school during the early and mid-1980s. Rich would lie in bed and talk to truckers who were driving along Route 495 using a CB radio. He would joke around and interrupt the truckers, who seemed confused by the interactions. I would laugh quietly to myself.

Rich-Pop Warner Football Mid 1970s

Rich played football on a Pop Warner youth football team while attending Grafton Elementary School in the mid to late 1970s. He played running back and was unstoppable.

Jim and Rich attended many Red Sox baseball games together. One afternoon, Jim, Rich and Mom were sitting at the dining room table watching the start of a Red Sox game. Jim noticed that there were plenty of empty seats at the stadium and asked Rich if he wanted to go to the game. Rich, around eight or nine, agreed, and Jim drove them to Fenway Park. They had a great time and only missed the first few innings. Occasionally, Jim and Rich would listen to their "super tape" cassette of assorted hit songs while driving to and from Red Sox games.

I took Rich to a Red Sox game in the mid-1980s. We sat close to where outfielder Jim Rice was positioned playing left field. There was a quiet moment during the game while the pitcher was talking to the catcher. Rich shouted out, "Jim Rice!" He looked right up at Rich, waved and said, "Thank you!" Jim Rice played for the Red Sox his entire sixteen-year career and was inducted into the Baseball Hall of Fame in 2009.

A similar experience happened in the late 1980s when I took Rich to a Patriots vs. Dallas Cowboys football game. We were sitting around the fifty-yard line behind the Dallas Cowboys bench, and at a quiet moment, Rich shouted out, "Great game, Irvin!" to Dallas Cowboys wide receiver Michael Irvin. He looked up at Rich, waved and said, "Thank you!"

As previously mentioned, a year after Dad's retirement from the FBI in July 1977, he went to work as a Security Supervisor with Raytheon Corporation. Dad, Mom, Paul, Neal, and Rich went to Saudi Arabia, where Dad was put in charge of security for the Raytheon employees living in the American Complex referred to as "Rayville." Rich was around eleven or twelve years old and attended the American School located inside the complex.

After about three months of cultural shock whenever they left the American compound, Dad and Mom decided it would be best if Mom returned to Grafton with Paul, Marie, Neal, and Rich. Dad finished his time in Saudi Arabia, as agreed in his contract, and flew back and forth to be with the family as much as possible. I'm sure he felt bad about the fact that he would be away from Rich and Neal, who were still young kids in elementary school. Dad asked me to do things with Neal and Rich when possible while he finished his contract. I was happy to see them return from Saudi Arabia.

L - R – Lois, Rich, Marie, Paul

Rich and many of his classmates would meet behind the Mart Department Store and ride motorized minibikes on and around a large sand pile. I had never been to the location but remember Mom telling him to be careful.

Rich and Neal attended many of the Grafton Fire Department barbecues that were held up the street at the fire station located off Grafton Center Common. I remember seeing both Rich and Neal running around and playing with friends at these events in the mid-to-late 1970s. John was a member of the Grafton Volunteer Fire Department and helped cook chicken at many of these events.

**John Sr. Ouellette on Left
Filming Football Game**

The Grafton Fire Department would have a fire safety day once a year and allow kids to climb up one of the fire truck rescue ladders and jump off the roof of the Mart Department Store into a hand-held safety net. I watched both Rich and Neal jump off the roof into the safety nets. John was among the members of the fire department holding the net. Dad filmed a few of their jumps with his Super 8 film camera.

Rich enjoyed playing the board games *Stratego*, *I Sunk Your Battleship*, and *Monopoly*. I played many two-and three-hour *Monopoly* games with Rich, Neal, and their friend Paul Holland.

I never liked or played video games. Rich and Neal had the Atari football game in the early 1980s and convinced me to play. They were great at maneuvering the joysticks and scoring touchdowns. I began

Rich & Mark 1980s

to play the game with Rich and Neal and had a great time. Occasionally, Paul Holland would come down, and we would play against each other. If you won a game, you continued playing someone else until you lost.

During a hot summer July day in the early 1980s, the Xtra-Mart Convenient Store offered small eight-ounce cups of Slush Puppies for five-cents. Rich, Neal, Paul Holland and I were having an Atari football tournament in our TV room. I drove down to the Xtra Mart and bought twenty cups. We drank those slush puppies so fast I needed to return three more times to stock up. The third time, I brought a large plastic pitcher and asked the girl behind the counter if she could fill the pitcher and charge me for however many cups she estimated would fill the pitcher. I also offered her a five-dollar tip. She would not honor my request, so I bought eighty cups and brought the slush puppies home in a box that was made to hold a case of soda.

Rich and I enjoyed watching M-TV in the early and mid-1980s. This was when video jockeys showed only music videos and nothing else. I became a dedicated Devo fan thanks to M-TV. Our band, *Slant 6 and the Jumpstarts,* had a video to our song *Pull the Plug* played a few times in the late-night MTV music video rotation.

Rich enjoyed fishing at Lake Ripple and Silver Lake. When at Cape Cod, he would fish off the pier at Smugglers Beach in South Yarmouth.

Rich played football and participated in track and field while attending Grafton High School between 1982 and 1986. In my opinion, Rich, who played defensive end, should have been playing at running back. I went to as many of his football games and track meets as possible. During his time playing on the Grafton High School football team, they won two Super Bowls.

Rich played on the St. Philip's Catholic Youth Conference basketball team for a few seasons during his high school experience. I was his coach and had a great time working with the team. He had a positive attitude, worked hard, and was friends with everyone on the team.

Rich and Mark Kaczynski worked together at Mayflower Moving Company for many years after graduating from high school. They were our dedicated "roadies" for our band *Slant 6 and the Jumpstarts*. This allowed them the opportunity to have access to our live performances.

Rich enjoyed going ice fishing. There were many cold winter days when I would be driving down Worcester Street and see Rich out on the ice as I approached Lake Ripple. On one occasion, the Worcester Telegram and Gazette published a picture of Rich out on Lake Ripple ice fishing on a cold winter day.

Rich attended many of the St. Patrick's Day Parades held in Worcester, Massachusetts. I would watch the local news in the evening to see if I could find Rich standing by the side of the road watching. While I never spotted him on the news, a few people I know said they saw him on TV standing on the sidelines of the parade.

There were a few occasions when I rented a house on Cape Cod for a week or two and invited Rich to stay with us. Rich was low-maintenance and fun to hang out with. Sometimes, my girlfriend Mary and I brought Rich along with us when we rented rustic cabins in the White Mountains of New Hampshire for a weekend. I clearly remember one of these occasions in 1983 while driving up to the mountains with Rich and singing along with David Bowie's hit song "Let's Dance" every time it was played on the radio.

If someone were to ask me which of the seven Ouellette children was the most easygoing and friendly, it would be Rich. I felt that Mom and Rich had a unique connection because he was the youngest of seven children. Jim and I still refer to him as "Baby Rich."

Rich & AnnMarie Wedding Day

Rich and his girlfriend AnnMarie were married in Las Vegas on April 17, 2007. Together, they continued to support AnnMarie's son, Nick, who was attending Assumption College in Worcester, Massachusetts.

Ironically, I taught Nick when he was in the eighth grade, attending Grafton Middle School. Nick is a gifted athlete who has been involved with a variety of professional and semi-pro football teams. Rich and AnnMarie would go to as many of his football games as possible or watch him play on TV.

Rich currently works for the Massachusetts Bay Transit Authority. Rich and AnnMarie enjoy taking vacations at beaches on Cape Cod and in Rhode Island. I look forward to talking with Rich or getting together when his busy schedule allows. Rich is an amazing brother. I am so proud of how he has navigated his way through life and how he is so willing to help others. I have no doubt Mom and Dad are proud of Richard and the amazing things he has accomplished in such a short time.

CHAPTER 27

Elisa Ouellette

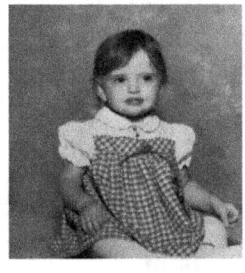

Elisa

Elisa was born on September 16, 1982, bringing a new dimension of joy and excitement into our family. She received a wealth of love and attention from her mother, my sister Marie, and our parents. In addition, Elisa had six uncles, John, Jim, Mark, Paul, Neal, and Rich, which meant there was never a dull moment in her early life.

Elisa was baptized at St. Philip's Parish in Grafton, Massachusetts, soon after being born. Sue Chartier, Marie's good friend, became her godmother, and I became her godfather.

Marie took Elisa shopping, to play at the Grafton "Super Park," on vacations to Cape Cod, on trips to visit relatives in Tennessee, to her soccer games, Silver Lake to swim, and Mass. She made sure that Elisa had wonderful Christmas experiences and birthday parties. We all enjoyed watching Elisa open gifts at these celebrations.

Marie kept Elisa up to date on the clothing fashions of the day. Elisa was the first "altar girl" to participate in a Mass at St. Philip's Parish. She was only ten years old and did a fantastic job. We were proud of her and looked forward to seeing her take part in Mass every weekend. Marie was an excellent role model. Mom was also involved with Elisa as a young child. She would take Elisa on day trips to Worcester when there was a day off from school. When I was working at the Opportunities Industrial Center in Worcester, teaching adult literacy, I would meet Elisa and Mom for lunch. Dad would put Elisa on his lap and read to her by the fireplace when she was a small child. He would read The Night Before Christmas to her between Thanksgiving and Christmas.

L - R Lois, Althea, Elisa, John Jr. – Late 1980s

Elisa liked to watch the television shows Zoom and Princess of Power. She had a friend named Katie who lived a few houses up the street. They would take turns going to each other's houses to play. Elisa would have "dance parties" in the living room in front of the fireplace while Dad relaxed and read books. She would recruit anyone who was home at any given time to watch her performances. Dad enjoyed taking her to Silver Lake in the summers, which is where she learned to swim.

FBI FAMILY STORY

On one occasion, my girlfriend Mary and I brought Elisa to the Grafton Flea Market when she was in a stroller. We also enjoyed taking Elisa to the playground when she was young.

At age ten, Elisa's friend Holly Piirainen was away on vacation with her family, staying at a cottage in Sturbridge, Massachusetts. On the morning of August 5, 1993, Holly was given permission to walk to a nearby neighbor's house to visit and play with their newly born puppies. Holly never returned home, and after about an hour, the family began searching for her and contacted the police.

Sadly, hunters discovered Holly's remains on October 23, 1993. The case is still unsolved. Although Dad had been retired from the FBI for sixteen years, Mrs. Piirainen asked Dad for his help with the investigation. I was not present during the discussion between Dad and Mrs. Piirainen, but I know Dad would have done anything and everything possible to help.

Elisa attended the Grafton Public Schools throughout most of her elementary and middle school years. Her high school experience was unique because her mother taught overseas for a long period. Elisa attended ninth grade at the Marymount International School in Rome, Italy, and participated in theater. She went to Grafton High School in Grafton, Massachusetts during her sophomore year and attended eleventh grade at Impington International Sixth Form College in England from September 1999 to December 1999 and Bahrain School (Department of Defense School) in Bahrain, Egypt from January 2000 to June 2000.

Elisa Ouellette

Elisa attended Grafton High School for her senior year and graduated on June 8, 2001. While at the American International School in Bahrain, Egypt, Elisa played the character Mimi in the play *Guys & Dolls*. She performed in the play on May 17, 2000, at the school. While attending Grafton High School, she was a member of the Chamber Choir. Elisa, like her mother, has an amazing voice. She had a lead role playing Laurey in the play, *Oklahoma*, her senior year. I remember attending all her performances with Dad.

Elisa has been involved with our band, *Slant 6 and the Jumpstarts,* for decades. She has performed many lead and backup vocals on our songs and has been fun to work with. There were many practice sessions when Elisa would show up to hang out and sing backup vocals. Elisa sang lead vocals on many of our original and parody songs that were incorporated into our album releases.

Elisa and I wrote and recorded a country-style song titled "Heading for Home," which received over 45,000 likes on "Jango-Radio." Jango-Radio is the largest internet radio station in the world, with over 800 million subscribers. She also performed vocals on our Christmas song, "It's Christmastime Everyone Everywhere," which continues to be played on internet radio stations during the holiday season.

Other *Slant 6 and the Jumpstarts* professional recordings Elisa has been involved with include, "Lonely Underground," "Don Knotts is Mick Jaggar's Dad," and "Police Got My Dad" a parody to "Feliz Navidad," to name a few. Elisa gave birth to her son Langdon on September 27, 2016. They live in Connecticut, where they focus on family and Elisa's career.

Epilogue

Writing *FBI Family Story* allowed me the opportunity to better understand why I have always cherished my childhood and the many wonderful experiences I encountered throughout my lifetime. I have few, if any, regrets and would do it over again if possible.

Yes, there were sad moments, but sadness is something everyone encounters at some point. My involvement with this project helped me to assemble and piece together the many amazing stories my parents shared with me over the years. How my mother was able to advance from a life of poverty to becoming an FBI file clerk was remarkable. Dad packed a lifetime of living into his first twenty-five years. He was a star athlete while in high school, graduated early to serve in the Army Air Corps near the close of World War II, earned his degree from Holy Cross, and began his amazing career with the FBI.

When my parents met at the FBI Headquarters in Knoxville, Tennessee, it truly was the beginning of an adventure that would span decades resulting in seven children, a unique family culture, and Dad's involvement with some of the most high-profile people and cases in America during the 1950s through the 1970s. The adventure continued for ten more years while working for Raytheon, following Dad's retirement from the FBI.

The most powerful insight I have gained while assembling this book is how important it is to understand our personal past, present, and future. My past is full of memories and life lessons that played a crucial role in who I have become today. The past is a fun place to visit when socializing with family and friends. The future continues to offer endless opportunities and dreams I can work toward and hope to fulfill during my lifetime yet; the future is not guaranteed.

What is most important is the present—right now. When you are blessed with the opportunity to wake up to a new day, be thankful and make the best of that day. A simple kind word or gesture is a powerful way to make any given day special.

Avon Lake, Ohio 1966

John Sr. at Sister Irene's Wedding

John Sr. with Parents

Irene, John Sr., Edna   **John Sr. with Parents & Sisters**

John Sr. with Family & Neighbors
Early 1930s

Lois & John Sr. Leaving for Honeymoon

Vegas 1957 Moving from NY to CA

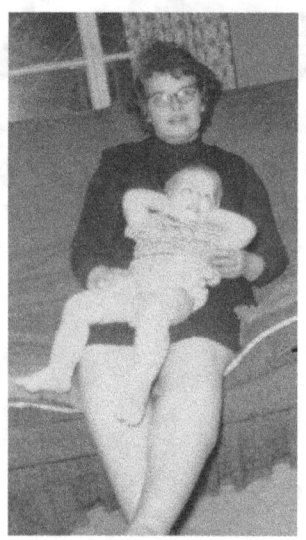

Lois holding Richard
Late 1960s

L - R Jack Morgan, Lois, John Sr. holding John Jr.,
Althea Morgan, Ron Duncan – Dayton, TN

Lois Empire State Bldg – NYC Honeymoon 1954

John Sr. Ouellette – Wedding Day 1954

L-R Irene, John Sr., Edna

John Sr. – Age 8

Irene & Edna

Kid Ouellette – Security Guard

John Jr., Jim – Halle Dept Store 1958

John Jr. Christmas 1957, Monterey CA

Early 1980s Ouellette Family

Christmas – Virginia Circle, Grafton, MA

L – R Neal, Marie, Paul, Mark, Jim, John
Avon Lake, OH

**Mr. & Mrs. Harrington -
Carol's Grandparents**

John Jr. Ouellette

L - R The Ouellette Children 1980s

Slant 6 and the Jumpstarts while Jim was in Alaska

L – R Mark, Mary, & John Ouellette Sr.

Family Gathering – Dayton, TN

Mark & Mary in Philippines – Adoption Sarah

Mark & Sarah – Age 6

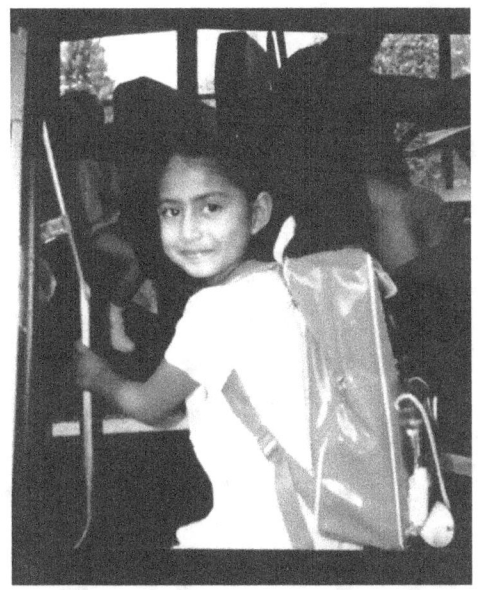

Sarah First Day of School – 1st Grade

Sarah – Age 6

Sarah & Mark

Sarah at Christmas – Early 2000s

**L - R Mark, Sarah, Mary
Sarah College Graduation**

Jim at Studio in Sutton, MA, Filming Promo Video for
Christmas Parody by Slant 6 and the Jumpstarts

Johnny, Julia, Jim, Sarah on Jim's Birthday

EPILOGUE

Julia

Johnny & Mark

Julia – Senior

John – Band

Mark & Carol at the Beach

Stone House Kettle Corn – Chester, VT

Mark & Carol – July 4, 2015

Carol & Emma Making a Snowman at Cape Cod House 2015.

Sarah & Kyle with Ella Mae

EPILOGUE

L – R Neal, Marie, Paul, Mark, Jim, John Jr. holding Richard

Ouellette Family Timeline

1926	John N. Ouellette born October 18.
1930	Lois Lillian Morgan born November 22.
1945	Dad graduates from North High School in Worcester, Massachusetts February.
1945	Dad enters active duty in the US Army Air Corps in February. Later transitioned into US Army.
1947	Dad receives honorable discharge from military and enters Holy Cross College in fall.
1948	Mom graduates from Rhea County High School in Dayton, Tennessee in spring.
1948	Mom begins training and becomes an FBI File Security Clerk in Washington, DC, then Knoxville, Tennessee.
1951	Dad graduates from Holy Cross College in spring, joins FBI and trains in Quantico, Virginia, then stationed in Detroit, Michigan.
1954	Dad transferred to Knoxville, Tennessee. Mom & Dad started dating.
1954	Mom & Dad are married June 20.

1955	Mom & Dad transferred to New York City. John born May 9.
1957	Dad transferred to Monterey, California. Jim born March 25.
1958	Dad transferred to Cleveland, Ohio. Lived in Parma, Ohio. Mark born March 1.
1959	Moved to 115th Street, Cleveland, Ohio. Paul born November 18.
1960/ 1961	Moved to Thoreau Road in Lakewood, Ohio.
1962	Marie born July 28.
1965	Moved to Avon Lake, Ohio. Neal born August 29.
1968	Richard born September 17.
1970	Dad transferred to Washington, DC in December. We moved to Lorton, Virginia.
1972	Dad transferred to Boston, Massachusetts in April. We moved to Grafton, Massachusetts.
1977	Dad retired from FBI July 30.
1978	Dad accepted job with Raytheon Company.
1988	Dad retired from Raytheon Company.
1995	Mom passed July 20.
1996	John passed April 1.
2015	Dad passed May 15.

About the Author

Mark Stephen Ouellette was born third among seven siblings to John and Lois Margan Ouellette, who met in 1952 at the Knoxville, Tennessee FBI Headquarters.

He attended Worcester State College during the early to mid-1980s, earning a Bachelor of Science (Sociology) and Master of Education (History) degrees. Mark spent over thirty years teaching special education and social studies in the private and public school sectors.

Now retired from the classroom, Mark continues to cultivate his creative spirit with his comedy/novelty rock band *Slant 6 and the Jumpstarts* and serves as product manager of Head Case Creations, LLC.

ABOUT THE AUTHOR

Mark finds joy and balance in an active lifestyle, indulging in his love for weightlifting, running, and biking while enjoying quality time with his girlfriend Carol, and his daughter, Sarah, her fiancé Kyle, and their dog Ella Mae.

Mark is available for book signing events, public speaking, media presentations, television, podcast, radio, telephone interviews, blog participation, and public guest appearances.

Contact: Mark Ouellette

PO Box 253

York Harbor, Maine 03911

https://fbifamilystory.org/an-fbi-family-story (website)

Facebook: Mark Ouellette

Instagram: fbi.family.story

https://www.instagram.com/fbi.family.story/

Acknowledgements

Thank you to all who contributed to this book in any way. Special thanks to Carol Ann Leofanti, who offered love, support, inspiration, and motivation throughout the entire book-writing process, and every day we have been together for the past twelve years.

I would like to acknowledge my siblings John, Jr., and the use of his personal files left in my dad's possession, James, who offered an abundance of information related to our parents and family, Paul, Marie, Neal, and Richard for their contributions, large or small.

Thank you to Cathy Harrington for Grafton historical contributions and my daughter Sarah Diza Ouellette for her inspiration.

I want to express my gratitude to Dottie Summerlin, President of the Mantua, Ohio Historical Society, and Harry Buchert for their contributions to my "Great UFO Chase" research, particularly regarding the photo taken in 1966 by Harry's father, Police Chief Gerald Buchert, of a UFO. My thanks also go to the Artis Mortis Gallery for the Zanesville, Ohio, UFO photograph. Special thanks to the Federal Bureau of Investigation for the public access to thousands of declassified documents available at FBI Records: The Vault.

Bibliography

Artis Mortis Gallery. *UFO Photo, Zanesville, Ohio, February 2, 1967 & UFO Identification Chart.*

Buchert, Gerald. *UFO Photo, April 17, 1966.*

FBI Records: The Vault. *Declassified Documents.*

Ouellette, James. Personal interviews and photos.

Ouellette, John Jr. Personal files, photos, documents, and notes.

Ouellette, John, Sr. Personal interviews, files, photos, documents, and notes.

Ouellette, Lois. Personal interviews, files, photos, documents, and notes.